THE SECRET BEHIND
SUCCESS

Vernessa
Thomas

ERIC THOMAS

SECRET TO
CCESS

The Promise Delayed Not Denied

Cover Design: Daryl S. Anderson, Sr.

Cover Photographer: Bruce Turner Photography

Editor: Darrian Tanner

Layout Design: OA.Blueprints, LLC

Printed in the United States of America

ISBN: 978-1-942499-09-1

PUBLICATIONS

CONTENTS

DEDICATION

This book is dedicated to my husband Jesse Thomas. I want to thank you for being that special person who saw my gifts through my hard exterior. You loved me although I was a work in progress. Your soft spoken demeanor and visions propelled us to heights I could have never dreamed of without you by my side. Thank you for being open minded enough to accept and love my son as your own. You are my soulmate, and I will always love you.

To my children, Eric, Jeneco and Mallori who inspired me to push forward so I could be a positive role model for you all! Together we changed our narrative. We are the first of my family to not only complete high school, but the five of us (including my husband) have all earned a college degree. I'm so proud of you guys, and I love you to the moon and beyond.

To my mother, Lama, thank you for raising me to be a strong, proud woman. Without the hardships in my youth, I would not have made it. You taught me to make something out of nothing. I am grateful to have had a mother like you. I too could see more clearly after I had children of my own. I love you so much.

To my sister Wanda, you are still my ride or die homie! Thank you for always being impartial and loving on me, Jesse and my 3 rugrats!

To DeeDee, I am humbly thankful for your help as I struggled to find my voice as I prepared to write my book.

To all those friends who kept me shored up when I was down but would not choose sides. I am truly grateful for your candor when the truth needed to be spoken! Much love ladies. And last but not least, I want to say thank you to our Heavenly Father who protected me during my trials and hardships by sending in his mighty Angels who shielded me and shed a light to guide me towards a safe harbor time and time again!

TESTIMONIALS

I would like to take this time to share some testimonies from some young people who have been a part of my life throughout the years.

I learned very early in life that the popular quote, "blood is thicker than water" isn't always true; however, the choice of love is. I first met Auntie Vernessa during a very scary time in my life. I was nine years old, and my youngest sister and I had been removed from our mother's custody because of her drug abuse. I remember being dropped off at Auntie Vernessa's home and being told that this was our new home, a foster home. I had heard only horror stories about foster homes and was terrified that we would not be treated right. Needless to say, we were treated wonderfully, and I can attribute where I am today to the lovingkindness of Auntie Vernessa. She opened my eyes to a world that I had never known and showed me the possibilities of what I could become.

It was in her home that I saw what a family could be and what true safety and consistency felt like. I had the opportunity to see, for the very first time in my life, what it was like to be wanted. She opened her home and shared her time with me. She invested in me so that I could get to where I needed to be. I remember taking classes in performing arts, food etiquette, and proper English and attending camps where I learned valuable life skills that I still use today. Years after leaving her home, most people could not believe the circumstances in which I grew up because I was so well versed because of the classes I mentioned above.

I've never met or heard of a person who maintains contact with previous foster parents such as I do, and I believe that says a lot.

Auntie Vernessa has helped me through college, supported me in marriage, and extended her love to my husband and daughter. She meets up with me when she is in my area. She makes a conscious effort to be a part of my life, and I'm truly thankful. It was unfortunate circumstances that connected us, but it is her sincere love for me that maintains our relationship. She is truly an amazing person, and in the near future, I hope to do the same thing she did for me by fostering children.
—Keysha Patterson

I can vividly remember February 2016 when I was preparing for a trip to St. Louis to attend the Average Skill Phenomenal Will Tour conference hosted by Eric Thomas. I purchased my tickets online and was overcharged by mistake. I had to call the ETA Customer Service line a couple of times to get my charges reversed. Every time I called, it was this same pleasant voice. The person at the other end of the phone was very nice. I called so many times that eventually I built a bond with this person over the phone. I didn't know that it was Eric Thomas's mom! It's so funny how we can disclose so much to a complete stranger without knowing that there is a divine purpose behind our meeting. She told me that everyone called her Ms. Vickie. She has been such an inspiration and an open book in my life thus far. As we were building our relationship, she shared some great things with me. We both became moms when we were teenagers, and I remember her telling me that we shouldn't allow that situation to prevent us from moving beyond our destiny.

On my journey to radiology school—a very competitive program that accepted only twenty-two students a year—I was rejected twice before getting accepted into the program and was then dismissed for an entire year. With her encouraging words in mind, I was still resilient enough to complete the program and to walk across the stage in May of 2017. Even after graduation, I hit another stumbling block when I failed my state boards twice. I was just one point away from passing on my second attempt. Yet Vickie

encouraged me to continue to study every day. She would say, "You have worked too hard not to get the prize." Our God is so phenomenal that we never know who he's going to place in our life, so we always have to be sweet to one another. It's so miraculous to build a connection with someone over the phone whom you've never met in person. Ms. Vickie, I want to thank you for all the time you took just to listen to me. The times you shared the challenges of being a single mom helped me to see my obstacles from a different view. You have given so much genuine advice to my children and me. I love you, and I support you. You are like the Auntie I never had. All glory to our Creator.
—*Angela West*

I can still remember my first encounter with Auntie Vernessa and Uncle Jesse. I was 12 years old and was experiencing behavior problems at school and home. My grandmother heard about the Michigan Respite Program and how it might help me through the rough emotional issues I was experiencing. My grandmother signed me up so that I could get some much needed rest from the issues at home. While Auntie cooked for us and loved on us, Uncle Jesse, as all the Respite kids called him, would hang out with us. Uncle J was the first man in my life who took time out for me. In their home, I learned family values, and I began to understand what a true friendship felt like. There, I had time for myself, and I could just be a kid! I remained with them for 3 years and to this day we still talk. I learned to be a real man and have managed to remain out of trouble.

They signed me up for the Boys and Girls Club and Science Club at Wayne State to keep me out of the streets. Uncle J. taught us to play cards and shoot pool, too. I have held on to the lessons I learned to this day! I have never gotten into any trouble.
—*Sean Finkley*

I met Mrs. Thomas when I was a young single mom. I was following up on a lead for an apartment for me and my young child. I was only nineteen, but Mr. and Mrs. Thomas took a chance on me and rented out the apartment to me. She explained that she too had been in the situation I was in, and she felt obligated to help, as someone had taken a chance on her years ago. While living there I became friends with her daughter, and she encouraged and helped me to get certified for a LPN program. Meeting them helped me change the course of my life. I paid it forward by helping other young ladies get through their challenges, so they too could provide a better life for their families.

-Rita Wright

INTRODUCTION

The Cat is Out of the Bag

There are times when life delivers us powerful, painful blows. I chose to bury mine because it was too painful to address at the time. I had a lot of the book sense as a teenager, but I didn't socially interact with people outside of my immediate family. My ignorance about sexual reproduction led me to engaging in unprotected sex at the age of 16 with a young man from my high school. I became pregnant. As I worked to figure out how I would cope with my pregnancy and the birth of my firstborn, I chose an attitude that screamed "let the dead stay buried." I worked with all of my might to keep my secret hidden. I placed all of the hurt and pain inside an iron clad vault burying it deep in my subconscious. After giving birth to Eric, I moved on with my life and managed to meet my future husband. After getting married and moving away from Chicago, I started to see this new journey as a way to start over. I could pretend that I didn't have a blended family. I could act as if I didn't have a secret that I was holding on to.

My shame was brought back to the forefront when my son published his first book, The Secret to Success. I managed to keep my secret from the public at large for many years. I was unable to read Eric's book for a long time because I felt it exposed my life as a lie. Although our story had many common elements because of our mother and son experiences, I felt that he was wrong to publish such personal information. The book would lay bare the lies I had managed to keep for so long. I felt justified with the secret, but there was only one problem with what I was trying to hide. In the words of a Mafia boss, "If two people know a secret, one has to die." Too many people became aware of my situation, so Eric would hear murmuring for many, many years before the day came when he finally asked me who was his real father.

Many years have passed since Eric's first book, and I am now ready to share some gems. I have finally found the freedom it took me so long to locate and grab hold to because I first had to be freed from the stigma I placed on myself. After I got over my own embarrassment of having my story published, I've realized there are secrets to overcoming any challenge that comes your way.

I've always mentored other young single moms, but this book is for mothers as well as fathers. It highlights the potential pain we can heap on our children because of the secrets we don't wish to reveal. My desire to erase my past led me to make a choice that created a storm. It was a storm that would emotionally impact Eric for the rest of his life. That choice was to raise Eric as Jesse's child without sharing information about his biological father. The secret was so deep that our two younger daughters were not even told that Eric was born outside of our marriage.

My story depicts my life and how we confronted the fallout of keeping Eric's true birth information from him. Most importantly it highlights how issues of this magnitude can be overcome with honesty and accepting responsibility. These two things were essential to repairing the relationship. I want you to use my challenges and the lessons that I share in this book as principles. Your situation doesn't have to be the same as mine, but the principles in my story will help you break free and remove those chains of shame, disappointment, and any type of mental and emotional bondage. You must understand that holding on to secrets will not allow you to be free, and if you aren't free you can't live up to your full potential. This book will show you how difficult life situations can be the push that carries you towards repairing relationships and the push that leads you into greatness.

PART I

BEFORE
THE SECRET

"Failure will not overtake me if my determination
to succeed is strong enough."
— *O. G. Mandino*

CHAPTER 1

Pregnant at Seventeen

After my swim class, I rushed to the shower so that I could leave school on time. I didn't want to miss my bus for work. Without warning, my swim coach, Mrs. Smith, barged into my dressing stall and yanked my towel off. She had suspected that I was pregnant. A few of my fellow peers caught me drying off after swim class so they must have told her what they saw. Later, I would learn that she asked those same girls to continue to follow me to the shower and dressing area until they had solid proof of my pregnancy.

My secret was exposed! Outing me was her malicious act of revenge.

I would never have expected for my pregnancy to be laid bare in such a painful public setting. The other swimmers, who were still in the changing room, pressed forward eagerly to witness her dish out my public degradation. Coach turned to my classmates after verbally attacking me, and she told them, "She is not worthy of being a student in our school." Coach Smith and my mother had a confrontation during my freshman year because she had paddled my sister and me so harshly that it left bruises on our bodies. It seemed as if she never forgave me or my sister for the scene my mother caused. I remember it like it was yesterday. The room was filled with students, and my mom threatened Coach Smith with bodily harm if she ever laid hands on us again.

Where did I slip up? I had been so very careful. The tight girdle should have hidden my growing belly so I could complete my last semester. I could not have factored in Coach's spies.

Her final words to me that day were, "I will see that you won't graduate." She then headed to the principal's office to start the dismissal process. I was scheduled to graduate in the class of 1970. I had already finished my course work, and my academic ranking had just been posted. I was scheduled to graduate in the top 10% of my class. She turned back to me once again with a smug look on her face to make her point; then she left the locker-room. Not one of the girls I had spent almost four years attending classes with came forward to console me. I was shell-shocked, still standing there wrapped in a wet towel. I couldn't believe what just happened. I was frozen and unable to get dressed until I saw the janitor beginning to gather up the wet school issued swimsuits and towels.

I was outed in a public, humiliating manner. It was right in front of my peers, and it destroyed the little self-esteem I was desperately clinging to. Somehow, I still managed to get a late bus to work. I needed time to wrap my head around what had just happened. I wondered if she could actually get me kicked out of school just because I was pregnant. I had no one that I could go to for comfort. My mom didn't know I was pregnant, and my boyfriend at the time, Gerald, had lied to me about using adequate protection so I didn't want to talk to him. I didn't think my father would offer any sympathy either.

Talk about rotten luck. During my senior year, I had finally found a job at a senior assisted-living complex called Chelsea House. I truly needed that job to earn bus fare to get to school. While it was a privilege to attend my high school Dunbar, there were costs associated with attending a school outside of my district. With my mom trying to take care of me and my 12 siblings, finding money for my bus fare was a constant struggle. I had to come up with my own money; mom could not afford it.

With being a part of such a large family, we didn't get allowances. I couldn't even afford to buy lunch at school. I was still packing lunch as a senior. It was embarrassing, so I usually ate my lunch standing at my locker. There were forms that low-income parents could complete to qualify for free lunch; the catch was everyone would know you received "free lunch vouchers" because there were certain food items you could not get for free. I was too ashamed to ask my mom to fill them out. Having funds to eat at the school cafeteria or the fact that I could buy a Vienna hot dog at the local stand kept me motivated to work. Being poor at my middle school wasn't so bad because most of the kids were in the same dire straits, but Dunbar was different. Securing an after-school and weekend hustle would change my financial situation for the better! So what if I was tired. I just needed to get adjusted to my new schedule—or so I thought.

I was determined to keep that after-school job even though it was a struggle. My mornings started before 5:30 a.m. I'd get up before my other sisters made their way to the bathroom. Getting up early was the only way to have any privacy with everyone sharing one bathroom! My routine was to get dressed, eat breakfast, and head out to the bus stop for school. Man, going to school full-time and working after class and most weekends was grueling. I would walk from 44th Place between Forestville and Vincennes to South Park Street where I would catch either the #3 South Park Bus line or hop into a jitney cab to ride to school.

Coach Smith made good on her promise to me. I was expelled just two months before my graduation, but my mother had not received the expulsion letter! I was hoping that Coach Smith would not follow through, so I returned to school the next day like nothing had happened. Mr. Chapman, my counselor, must have heard that I was on the school grounds because he came looking for me. He pulled me aside and asked why I was back in the building. He said that he knew what had happened in the locker room. I told him that my mom had not gotten a phone call or notice of me being expelled.

He said, "Vernessa, you can't attend class here anymore. The School Board has rules that forbid pregnant students from attending schools. You can't remain here."

He then added on, "With your grades being so high, you can still graduate. I just can't adjust the rules to keep you as an active student here." With his help in explaining the rules and regulations required for graduation, I was able to do just that! I would not allow that mean, vengeful teacher to steal my future from me by forcing me to leave school when I was so close to finishing just because I was pregnant. Coach Smith knew my ranking as well as the rules, but she chose to withhold that important information from me. She wanted to ruin me and thought that after being the target of her shameless behavior I would lie down and quit. I could not have believed that a grown woman—and a teacher at that—would be so petty and vindictive.

Days before being outed in the locker room I noticed that I was unusually tired all the time, but I thought it was due to my heavy class load. I had been complaining about my lack of energy for a while, but I blamed it all on my grueling class schedule. On top of my class load I had finally found a part time job, working after school three to four days a week. My period was irregular, but it never alarmed me because I was spotting a little.

With all of those elements combined with running out of school every day so I wouldn't miss the bus, I was not concerned about my lack of stamina! During a super busy shift at work, I actually ran out of steam and had to sit down as I complained about being exhausted. This was the first time the thought of being pregnant entered my mind. One of the senior employees said, "Chile, you ain't tired. You pregnant." She went on to say that she had seen too many pregnant women to not recognize it for what it was. Up until that point, it had never entered my mind that I might actually be pregnant! At the Chelsea House, as the new hire, I substituted or floated whenever they needed my help. I wanted to work twenty hours a week, so I would call in every day on my lunch break to see if I had made the schedule for that day. Being worn out seemed logical, so I never gave it a thought.

How was I pregnant? My boyfriend always used protection; he promised it would stop me from having a baby! What a fool I was to keep repeating that over and over in my head.

Driven by my emotions, I immediately shut down and went into a state of denial. Having a baby at 17 would be the death of my plans and dreams to escape my current situation. I thought my plans for escaping 43rd Street and getting into college would be over.

I was disappointed with myself. I became disgusted in just thinking about what my teachers and counselors would say when they found out about the secret that I was carrying. I suffered from anxiety and fear, yet I still did not tell my mother. My brain didn't want to accept it even as my belly began to bulge.

All I could think about was how my being pregnant at seventeen would be the death of my plans and dreams to escape from poverty, to get away from all those beaten-down people, and to rid myself of a life of deprivation. I was so disappointed with myself. I had witnessed too many women in my neighborhood have that first baby and then a second one and then another until they became trapped in a downward spiral of poverty. I watched them lose their desire for a better life because the welfare train was so easy to jump on and ride! The young ones couldn't see that welfare was actually a prison system leading to a lifetime of dependency. They couldn't see that when the last child turned eighteen, funding would stop. Therefore, they would be thirty-five or older without the skills to create a decent life for themselves.

My own mother would go through this cycle of dependency. She had fourteen live births, and it sucked the life out of her dreams and plans to move forward to a better life for herself. As I accepted the words from my co-worker, I was consumed with worry. As I said before, I did not tell my mother or share my condition with anyone else for months. I put my unborn child in peril because I wasn't able to seek prenatal care while carrying my lie. I weighed only 114 pounds! I don't know how it wasn't obvious to other people, even though I purchased the tightest girdle I could find to keep my pregnancy hidden. I was in denial. I could not accept that I was having a baby. Accepting it meant giving up on my plans for a better future.

Mama Knows Something
Now my mama didn't miss much about her children. She seemed to have had a third eye to keep tabs on what we were up to. I was always on the edge wondering when she would finally confront me. My mom eventually found out in the most unorthodox way. Even though she had five teenaged daughters who were having their cycles, at some point she realized we weren't using the normal amount of feminine supplies. I suppose she set aside so much money to keep her girls properly supplied. She had shared with us that her grandmother made her use rags, and she would not allow us to use that method when we had our periods. She wasn't spending as much as she normally did, so she knew something was wrong. After grilling my older sisters, she eventually found her way to me and asked me if my period was late. I refused to

own up to being pregnant, all the while looking her straight in her eyes. It was a dumb move on my part. She called my bluff. My mama didn't take no mess. She said, "A liar is no better than a thief." She then just walked over to the phone and made an appointment for my first visit to a gynecologist.

The look in her eyes after she scheduled my appointment was a combination of absolute disbelief and utter disappointment towards me. She had known in her heart that I was the one who would make it out. I was her "good, smart, and wise daughter."

It became clear after our visit to the gynecologist that her greatest fear was realized. After that long wait to actually see the doctor, being exposed was a relief in some ways. I was suffocating under her cold, passive rejection. The doctor told her I was about twelve weeks along. I had carried so much stress by lying and hiding that I was exhausted! I later realized that Mama was slow in noticing my condition because she was pregnant as well. She was carrying her fourteenth child who was born just a short time after Eric.

My Daddy Ain't Dead

During my pregnancy, I reached out more to my biological father. He was not in our lives when we were young, but we became re-acquainted when I was just entering junior high school. When we asked our mom why our brothers and younger siblings' father wasn't our father too, she told my sisters and me that our dad was dead. Try to imagine my disbelief when he came back into my life one random Saturday morning in 1962 during summer break. His wife was in tow.

As I recall, I was around ten years old. I'm not sure how he found us because there had been a fire in our previous apartment, and we had just relocated. We all watched him look from our eldest sister to the other five girls. He knew Glenda was one of his because she was his female 'mini-me'. He knew Wanda was as well because she had his light complexion. I can recall him turning his gaze to my two other sisters and me, trying to decide which of us belonged to him. My stepmother, who was wide-eyed and nervous, was standing there waiting to see who was who as well! I was the shortest of all the remaining girls which complicated things. He had not seen us for many years. My mother fidgeted because she knew that she had told us that he was dead. After a long, tense silent moment, she looked at me and said, "She's yours." I was identified as his third child.

Because I had truly accepted that he was dead, I had a difficult time connecting with him. But after many weekend visits over summer breaks, we slowly bonded and remained close until his death in 2001. My father had recently moved to Gary, Indiana and worked as a millwright at the Great Lakes Steel Mill. His wife was kind and always treated me well. The two of them were a Godsend during my pregnancy. My father wanted me to come live with them, but I wasn't able to transfer to a school in Gary because I was in my senior year. My dad provided some funds which allowed me to pay my prom and school fees so that I could graduate. Bernice, my stepmother, always snuck in a little extra money. My son's paternal grandfather talked to his mom, and she agreed that I could move in with her after I graduated. Between my father and especially Eric's paternal grandfather and great-grandmother, I had a wealth of support which provided a temporary refuge and whatever I needed to keep going.

I made Mr. Chapman, my counselor, become proud of his decision to be my voice when I was too young and uninformed to know that what was happening to me was illegal and unethical. I used my graduation from Dunbar Vocational High School as my stepping-stone to fulfill my original dream. Although there were delays along the way, I made good on the promises I made to my younger self! I had made it after all. I earned my certificate in printing, and I was actually on my way to graduating.

Gerald Finds Out
I was still hiding the pregnancy from my boyfriend. I was so bit-

ter that he had lied to me about using the proper protection. My fear of being an unwed mother drove me crazy. The women at work encouraged me to tell him, but I was too angry, scared, and ashamed.

A blow up with my mother forced my hand. The physical work involved in going to school and working three or four days a week took its toll on me. I gave my two-week notice, and I quit the job. When my mother realized I was coming home after school and wasn't working, I told her that I couldn't do it and that I quit my job. She asked, "How are you going to find bus fare to get to school?" I was finally forced to call Gerald, my boyfriend. I broke down and told him everything. I had started missing school because I didn't have bus fare once all my funds ran out from working. My mother could not come up with the money. He never knew that I paid for my own bus fare.

Gerald's father got involved when he realized I would be forced to stop school if I couldn't attend and that I was carrying his grand-child. He let Gerald drive his car so that I would not miss any more school. He also made sure to stop by my school most weeks to give me a few dollars, but I was still humiliated that my mother could not provide for me during my time of need. I was ashamed that I had to turn to someone outside my family for my basic needs. Mr. Mundy, Gerald's dad, not only came through for me then, but he convinced his mom, Louise Jones, to take me in after I graduated! Things did not get better at home. My mother's continuous pas-sive rejection had a huge bearing on my decision to accept Mr. Mundy's offer of a place to stay. Mom only spoke of her aspira-tions for me and how she was devastated and disappointed that I had made the same mistakes she had. I left home bitter and de-feated. I could not forgive my mother for the way she had failed to support me in my time of need. I didn't understand how she could behave toward me in such a mean-spirited way, especially since she was pregnant as well.

Prom Night

Being banished from high school was one thing, but attending my prom was another. Not surprisingly, Gerald and I were already experiencing issues. He had dropped out of high school during his senior year. His being absent during my time of need became a sad refrain early on in our relationship. However, because I would be able to walk across the stage on the graduation day, I wasn't totally devastated. I was able to see that all of my dreams didn't have to end just because I was having a baby. I finished high school, and that had allowed me to walk across the stage with my classmates because I listened to my angels, like Mr. Chapman, who showed me how to negotiate, the school system. We all have guardian angels; we just need to listen to that still quiet voice that gives us direction and advice.

I was told that my school had no jurisdiction regarding the prom. My stepmom convinced me to attend my prom, so we went looking for a dress that would hide my growing belly. We finally settled on a turquoise empire-waist dress with satin shoes and a purse dyed to match. But there was only one problem. I didn't have a date! My humiliation level was maxed out with how our relationship had imploded so there was no way I would be able to pretend things were good between Gerald and me. I wasn't going to do that just so I would have a date for the prom.

So much support came by way of my kind neighbors. They made me feel like I still mattered. They had dreams and aspirations rid- ing on me! The ladies would say, "You're not like the rest of the children." They told me that they thought I was going to be somebody. They all rallied behind me, even as my mother continued to push me away. They said, "You're going to go to your prom, and you're going to graduate and walk across that stage in your cap and gown with that big belly!"

On prom night, a group of older women from across my block summoned me over and began helping me to get ready. I was rocking my Afro, trying to look like Angela Davis at the time. Many of the older people didn't like the young people wearing the natural look. Ms. Stella told me directly, "You are not wearing no nappy head tonight." She sat me down in the kitchen next to the gas stove that had a pressing comb heating up. Next to the comb was a can of bergamot hair grease melting from resting near the hot stove. She began straightening my hair. After she got it straightened to her liking, she brought out several of her own clip-on cascade hairpieces and told me to pick out the one I liked. I made my selection, and she clipped it in place along with many bobby pins to keep my real hair in place. She fussed the entire time, but I knew it was just her way of expressing her love. Another lady lent me a pair of fancy clip-on earrings, and one painted my nails. My amazing village came together that evening to see that I was dolled up properly! An older neighbor whose skin tone was close to my skin tone brought over her own pressed powder, sponge, and rouge. She proudly made me up as she said, "I am going to get you right for your prom." Another lent me her tube of lipstick.

I was Cinderella that evening! In spite of my dismal situation, I felt worthy and valued by all the love directed towards me! As they continued to pamper me, one of the ladies took pictures with her Polaroid camera. I was floating on a cloud of love. At the last moment, my brother-in-law, Jimmy, stepped in as my borrowed prince. He escorted me so that I wouldn't experience my senior ball all by myself. Jimmy had been a Dunbar Mighty Man too; he said that he had to represent our school! Even though my mom saw my situation as a cup half empty, my beloved neighbors taught me to see it as a cup half full. They all said, "It happened. Now you go out there girl, and live your life. We will continue to rally behind you." And boy, did they ever!

Reality was suspended for a short time. My stepmother made sure that my dad sent money for my prom pictures. I'm telling you that night was magical. I'll never forget how my block stood behind me! I didn't know how my classmates would react to my pregnancy, but they were not judgmental. Most had heard about the shower scene, and Coach's minions faced much shaming. Everyone was happy that Mr. Chapman had been able to mitigate most of her malicious actions. One of my fellow peers pulled me aside and told me privately that just as she was graduating in June, she had a five-year-old daughter who would be entering kindergarten that fall. Her family had rallied behind her.

Just as for Cinderella, the clock struck midnight, and everything faded to black—but not before I was also able to walk across the stage and receive the diploma that I had worked so tirelessly to earn. Our incoming 1966 class was the biggest ever, with just a fifty percent graduation rate. The fact that I endured all of my trials made it all the more precious!

Mother 2 Mother: Pregnant at Seventeen
I had been so ashamed to face the world because I was cast in an unsavory light by the so-called moral majority, but I knew getting my diploma was the first step towards landing a decent job. I squared my shoulders and returned to my high school, praying it was all a bad dream!

Mr. Chapman saw my determination, and he shared precious information that overrode my teacher's plans. I didn't know it then, but I was just like my classmate who had a child at 14 or 15 years old. She pressed through no matter the landmines that were in her way, and she graduated! She shared her journey, and it gave me the strength and determination to press on. She and I both proved that a setback was only a comeback!

LESSONS LEARNED

- If or when your original plans get derailed, it's time to create a Plan B, C or whatever it takes to get your life back on track.
- I got my life together because I feared my son would have the same life I so dearly resented–a life of lack!
- If there was to be a better life for us, then tag–I was it!
- When my son became of age, I made sure he understood everything about birth control. I wanted him to be able to make informed decisions once he decided to become sexually active so that he could protect himself from becoming a young father.
- You are NOT your current situation.
- Stop playing the "victim." Get out of your feelings. You must own it in order to move ahead.
- If you let someone else make possible life altering decisions for you, don't do the blame game.
- Become proactive and protect yourself from further "accidents."
- Don't let society decide what will become of you because you are a single mom.
- Bringing a life into this world can be that motivation you need to push yourself to great heights.

CHAPTER 2

Things Get Worse at Home

Prom and graduation were over with and done. I was now trapped at home all day and every day without anything constructive to do. With my Dad often working seven days a week and my stepmother unable to drive to Chicago to pick me up, I wasn't able to escape home. Whenever I asked Gerald to come get me and drop me off at my Dad's home, he demanded gas money which he knew I seldom had. What a prince!

Just try to imagine two pregnant women, both miserable, in sweltering heat and with no air conditioning. It was a recipe for disaster. Neither, time nor the fact that I graduated without having to attend summer school improved the relationship between my mother and me.

At this point I was almost six months into the pregnancy. My mother would have been about three and a half months along with my baby sister, Kim. All I can really remember is just trying to stay out of her sight. I could not do anything right in her eyes that summer. I experienced extreme morning sickness and was sleeping like crazy, which was to be expected, but even that didn't sit right with her. Looking back, my adult self could see that Mama always set me apart in so many ways. I was bright and loved to read; I was a good daughter. It must have really knocked her off her rocker to see me fall so low in her eyes.

During that time, all I felt were waves after waves of sadness. Mom could not even be there for me during my trying times. In the early stages of my pregnancy, I was added to my mother's welfare case. After I finally left, I went to the welfare office to open my own case for my unborn child and myself. Growing up, I was always ashamed of being on the welfare rolls. However, in my current situation, it was a blessing to have our basic needs met—a blessing that I vowed to use only for a short while. I used what little cash they gave me to begin purchasing clothing and little things that I would need for my child. I knew I had to prepare as much as possible before the actual delivery. Because I could not drive, I knew that it would be a nightmare if I did not have things in place before my baby came. My father and stepmother agreed early on to purchase the bassinet, layette, and bedding. With my limited amount of cash, I requested only cloth diapers. At this point, I was spending quite a bit of time at my dad's place just to get away from all the stress of being home. My stepmother had two grown sons, but she was estranged from them. She never saw her biological grandchildren so I suppose becoming a grandmother to Eric made her proud, even under the current circumstances. She would make my dad control himself and not be so mean to me. When he lost his temper, I can recall her saying, "Vernessa is just in the kitchen, so she can hear you. There's no need to make her feel any worse."

In the summer of 1970, we experienced record high heat and had no access to air conditioning. Traveling between Gary, Indiana, Eric's great-grandmother's home, and my mother's house was taking a toll on both my emotional and physical health. My weight had ballooned from 114 pounds to 160 pounds. I was miserable, anxious, and depressed. At some point, I got too big to be on the road all the time. It was time to take Louise up on her offer to live with her full time. I spoke with my mom once more before leaving. I was hoping she would soften her stance; she did not. She said that moving in with Louise was my best option. I left my home and family with a heavy heart. We were still at odds, and she had not yielded one bit. I slowly transitioned from short stays at various homes and moved into Louise's home.

Because it was Gerald's grandmother's home, he had free rein so he often dropped by even though we were no longer a couple. I was only there because Gerald's father spoke on my behalf. I think I was at Louise's home about eight weeks before my labor pains began. After I left home, my mom and I rarely talked. Grandma Cleo was Gerald's maternal grandmother, and she was the caretaker for Louise's aunt so I always had a loving elder to guide me and help me cope with my pregnancy issues. I woke up with pain in my lower back one morning while she was working. Cleo noticed that I was bent over as I was walking, and she asked me what was going on and if the baby was coming. I remember telling her that the baby wasn't coming and that my stomach wasn't hurting. I just had some pressure in my lower back. Based on what I saw my older sisters suffer through during their labor and deliveries, I was not concerned about going into labor. However, by chance, Gerald had stayed overnight in a spare bedroom. Grandma Cleo decided to wake him up and tell him that the baby might be coming! I argued that she was overreacting. I was not experiencing any real pain. At some point, she insisted that her grandson get me down to Michael Reese Hospital where I was scheduled to give birth. Because of our ongoing estrangement, I didn't bother to reach out to my mother to let her know I was in labor. In my heart, I felt she had written me off!

We lived in the Chatham District, so it took about 20 minutes to get to the maternity ward. Gerald drove me down to the hospital without an incident, but as soon as we got on the elevator, my water broke. Upon exiting the elevator, I was whisked to the labor and delivery unit where the nurse began to prep me for my delivery. By then, the lower back pain had moved to my gut. I felt myself straining and grunting at this point. I was yelling to the nurses to let me up so that I could go to the bathroom. One nurse demanded loudly, "Stop pushing and start panting! Stop pushing now! That baby is coming!"

They rushed me into the delivery room. It was such a wonderful relief to be there. It had to be hotter than hell that day. The temperature in the birthing room was probably 66° F. It felt like heaven; the delivery room was so cool without the lingering muggy humidity. I sighed and rolled over to my right side so that I could get some much-needed rest. I was not concerned about having a baby at this point; I just wanted to go to sleep. It was cool, and it felt wonderfully refreshing. I can remember having to take my feet out of the stirrups. I must have been delirious; I don't know why because I hadn't been given any drugs. When I was examined, I was already at ten centimeters—too far gone to get any medication. I could hear the doctor through the fog telling me to put my foot back in the stirrup, and I felt him grabbing my leg, gently putting it back in place.

Well, I wasn't having it. I turned back over to my right side to sleep. The doctor grabbed my foot again but forcefully this time. He was yelling, but it was still just so blissfully cool. I wasn't trying to do anything but get some much-needed sleep. I did not cooperate at all! My son was delivered with forceps; I did not participate at all. Cool temps equaled sleep, restful sleep. I woke up some time later to a bunch of angry nurses admonishing me and asking me how did I have the "audacity" (their words) to ask them why my son's cheeks were so bruised and bloody. You may not believe it, but all the attending nurses cursed at me and called me out of my name! I couldn't believe it.

"What did I do so wrong that you feel you can speak to me like that?" I asked.

"You created complications by going to sleep. Your muscles didn't push your son out, and the doctor had to use forceps to get him out," the head nurse said.

They told me Eric was lucky because some infants suffered serious cranial damage from a forceps delivery. I was just a kid. Who knew? Thankfully, there was no long term damage, and the bruising faded away after a while. I tried, but I couldn't make them understand that nobody would go to sleep during childbirth unless they couldn't help it. They did not accept my apologies, and I remained under their bad grace for the entire three days and nights that I remained in the hospital. I found out the hard way that nurses gossip across shifts.

Eric was born within two hours and ten minutes after my first pain. After my troubled pregnancy, his arrival was a welcomed blessing. After we were discharged and sent home, my dad and step mom stopped by with the bassinet, sheets and blankets, booties and caps, and all the other things that a newborn should have. I had never had a baby shower, so there was not much stuff for Eric's homecoming. I am forever indebted to Bernice McWilliams, my stepmother, for her continued kindness. Louise Jones and her son Ernest Mundy provided many beautiful things for Eric as well. Grandma Cleo was always available to provide great parenting advice and to help keep my spirits up. However, although we had a gorgeous, safe place to lay our heads, I knew it wasn't an emotionally stable environment. Gerald's grandparents took care of anything we needed, but I can't recall him personally ever doing anything for me or for Eric—not even the basic things that every newborn needs.

LESSONS LEARNED

- False pride and stubbornness are counterproductive.
- In order for people to come to an agreement, someone has to yield.
- Sometimes you have to swallow your pride.
- If you don't have any leverage, you must learn to negotiate in order to get some of the things you need.

CHAPTER 3

My First Betrayal

I received several baby gifts from family and friends, but Gerald presented another kind of "gift" for me shortly after we were released from the hospital. We went back to stay at Grandma Louise's home. Eric was the first male grandson on his father's side, so I was forced to smile and be polite to the various friends and family members who came to see him. Gerald was as proud as a peacock as he and his dad examined Eric, pointing out the similarities among the three generations of Mundy men. Most guests would have been shocked to know it was all a façade.

One day a lady by the name of Fanny dropped by to see Eric within a few days after I was discharged. I knew her because she was the girlfriend of Gerald's best friend, Teddy. I recalled being curious about why Teddy wasn't with her that day. I soon discovered that she and Teddy were no longer an item.

She exclaimed how handsome Eric was and that she was so happy for me. Then unexpectedly her demeanor turned sour. She dropped her head as she quietly said, "I am also carrying Gerald's child. My child will be his second one."

I thought, "Where in the hell did this come from? Could my situation get any worse?"

Teddy had been Gerald's friend for many years, and Gerald was sleeping with his girl! I have no words to express how this bombshell made me feel. While it was clear that we weren't going to work through our problems, Gerald's lack of integrity left me shell-shocked. I remained in his grandmother's house by sheer force of stubbornness. His family had put me under the spotlight by declaring that their home was the best place for Eric and me. Of course, my pride played a role too. I would not return home to my mom without an apology from her! Where else could I go? To whom could I turn to?

Why would Gerald have allowed Fanny to come over so soon when I was trying to adjust to my role as a new mom? Would she be given the same considerations I received? Would Grandma Louise allow her to move in as well? In my heart of hearts, I knew she could not deny her son or grandson anything they asked of her. My thoughts were spinning like a Category 7 tornado.

The Fight
I decided to stay, but I held Gerald in contempt. During these dark days, I continued to question my own intelligence and character. How could I have been wise enough to stay away from the gangbangers and thugs in my own neighborhood but not be able to see this man for who he truly was? This did not sit well with Gerald; he became more and more mean-spirited as time went on. This led to heated arguments that often took place in front of his friends and Grandma Cleo.

The tension escalated into a terrible fight after one of his particularly mean-spirited displays. Early one morning, all of my pent-up anger and disappointment came to a roiling boil. My days always began with Cleo pulling out the Folgers and measuring out enough grounds for our daily pot of coffee. This was after first checking on her ward and her first great-grandson. She filled the percolator and set it on the stove to brew until it was a rich, dark brown. The physical fight with Gerald began just after she and I finished our first cup. Our argument intensified, and he pushed me toward the opening into the kitchen, showing off for his friends who had followed him home from an outing the night before. As I stumbled, he hurried towards me. I was close to the stove, so I reached up and grabbed the coffee pot and pitched the still-hot liquid at him. I then proceeded to strike him with the coffee pot. The coffee grounds flew everywhere, forcing him onto the back porch.

For a moment, Grandma Cleo just watched us tussling; she was in stunned silence. After what seemed an eternity, she quietly told Gerald to leave and to not come back into the apartment but to go down the back staircase. "Stay away," she admonished him. His friends escaped through the front entrance. They scurried down the stairs to meet back up with Gerald. He was the only one at the time who seemed to own a car.

Worriedly, Cleo then turned towards me to be sure I had not suffered any injuries.

"I'm okay," I said.

Grandma Cleo then said, "We have to get this place cleaned up before Louise gets home." We started cleaning the flecked wallpaper in the dining room and wiped down the walls that were generally eggshell white but now displayed streaks of a gritty sepia tone. As we cleaned, we both prayed that the stains would come out completely. Then we tackled the kitchen. We were scrubbing walls and wiping down anything that sported a coffee stain. After we finished, Cleo suggested we go over everything again to make sure we had covered our tracks. During the melee, it seemed that somehow a window had cracked noticeably. After much debate, we decided to blame the cracked window on the old woman stumbling on a throw rug. She was in her late eighties, so it seemed a plausible reason. Louise questioned Cleo's level of care, but she seemed to buy her excuse.

Later, Louise found out the real reason for the broken window from her beloved grandson. She wasn't happy when she asked why he hadn't been visiting as often. Once the truth came out, it meant that Eric and I had to leave her home—immediately. I was there because her son had petitioned her to allow me to stay there; she had only complied because it would please him. She made it clear to me that the only reason why we were allowed to live there was because her son asked her. It was never about us. I knew it was wrong, but I refused to leave. I told her, "We are not leaving. I can't go back home. I made the decision to leave my mom's home, and I am not going back. You will not put us out right now. We have nowhere to go."

It's Time to Go
Tensions mounted whenever Gerald was there, so he rarely stayed long. After we had another fight, it was time for me to pull up my big-girl panties and find a new apartment. I started looking for a place for Eric and me. I had never told anyone other than my partner in crime, Wanda, that I was receiving aid, so I still had some cash as well as all my food stamps from my welfare stipend.

As I was quietly plotting my move, Michael, Gerald's brother, came over. He pulled me aside and whispered, "You know I'm a post office worker. My route includes your sister Wanda's neighborhood. I deliver your check to her house." I was mortified. What would Mike do with that information? Was he going to blackmail me? He paused dramatically and then said, "I know my brother doesn't treat you and Eric right, and I promise you I will never tell him about this." My heart almost burst with joy! My plans were saved by his goodness toward us! Michael passed away with my secret many years later.

One afternoon I was feeling constricted. Since the blow up and my refusal to leave, the house was like a tomb after Cleo left for the evening. She only worked Monday through Fridays. On one of those blue Saturdays, Eric and I took the bus to Evergreen Plaza just to escape the gloom. I took some of the money I had been saving to shop for a few things for the two of us. Gerald had come to the apartment while we were out, so upon our return he noticed all of the shopping bags. He commented that I had spent quite a bit of money. He asked me where I had gotten the money; he had the audacity to rummage through my dresser while we were out. I was finally busted, I thought! I lied, and to justify my purchases, I told him that I had found a wallet earlier in the week when Eric and I had taken the bus to a doctor's appointment. He bought my excuse! I was almost hyperventilating as he mentioned that there was still almost twenty-five dollars in a sock in one of my drawers. Was that all he had found? Or was he lying?

I placed the bulk of the funds as well as the food stamps I received each month under the dresser drawer. I would pull the drawer off its track and line up my cash and food stamps in the hollow space beneath the tray upon which the drawers sat. I prayed that Gerald had not had the sense to look any further after discovering the money in the sock. He hadn't. I think that because of the way I acted, he probably thought I was broken and too weak to find a way out of that life in which I had found myself experiencing. I didn't appear to react right away to his rifling through my personal belongings; instead, I told him how lucky I was to have found the wallet. I told him that it seemed as if he wasn't going to ever get a job to help provide for the son that he was always bragging about. After my teasing, he got upset and left my room. I locked the door and pulled the drawer out without making a peep. My stash was still hidden!

There was always tension and stress between Gerald and me. There was no way I was going to continue down the path that I had seen my mom and so many of our friends' parents travel through. This would not be my story.

I had grown up in a home filled with fighting and arguing. I had seen those behaviors destroy so many women who took beatings and abuse because they felt they had no other option. I didn't want that for myself. I promised myself that my son would not be exposed to that kind of life. Gerald soon left after our latest battle. He always cut and ran which was easier than accepting some responsibility for the situation we had found ourselves in. I sat down to calm myself down and realized I was still there due to my false pride. This was it. It was time for us to move on. I called the only person who would move mountains for me, and that was my older sister Wanda. She was my #1 supporter. I told her what had happened and that our arguments were getting more physical. I was not going to be a battered woman, and I was not willing to do time in jail or prison for fighting back!

Wanda's husband, Jimmy, was at work. She called his workplace immediately and told him that there was an emergency and that she needed him to leave work and come pick her up! Wanda was ready for battle when she called back. She and Jimmy scooped me up within an hour. With Wanda's help, our move went off without a hitch. Everyone pitched in and quickly gathered up our stuff. I also called Grandma Cleo to get her blessing.

It took us two trips to load up and transport our stuff because Wanda and Jimmy had to bring their two little ones along. I made certain to clear out all of Eric's belongings as well. We were never coming back.

I experienced so many issues of betrayal with Gerald's lack of morals and consideration. Dealing with a man who felt that his own needs came first caused me to develop a great deal of mistrust in men and people in general. Eric's grandparents, who had been so generous to us as I went through my pregnancy and the birth of Eric, were no longer around. It became clear that their support was conditional because after the breakup, their assistance ended. I was so happy to move to my sister's house because Eric and I were welcomed there. We were received with love, and this lifted a heavy load from my mind and heart.

Knowing that I was leaving Eric in a healthy environment, I sought seasonal work and temporary jobs. Later, I was ready for my own place—somewhere I could leave my stuff and not feel like a visitor. I was too young to rent an apartment for myself, especially with a child. After living with my sister and family for many months, I finally got the nerve to ask if she and Jimmy would vouch for me so that I could get a studio apartment in Mrs. Hill's apartment building. Mrs. Hill had rented out their first apartment to them, and they still maintained contact with her. The two of them went to speak to Mrs. Hill on my behalf, and she said that she would rent out an apartment to me! Through their good word, I was able to rent a small studio apartment for my son and me.

I began to date another guy, and I experienced the same conditional relationship issues. He wanted to get closer to me, but he had a secret motive in thinking that I could help him pay off his bills. I recognized the patterns of manipulation and ulterior motives in men who "wanted" to be with me so I shut down and stopped dating. I began to look inside myself to identify and understand why I was attracting these unsavory guys. It was something about me and my brokenness that was causing this to happen.

LESSONS LEARNED

- Everything that glitters isn't gold. Be careful not to find yourself in a beautiful prison.
- At some point you must find some courage and prepare to leave an unhealthy relationship or environment.
- Remaining in a toxic environment can become your offspring's "normal" if you stay too long.
- Stop operating on an emotional level. It blinds you, and you won't be able to see all of the people and resources out there that can help you.
- Don't let your shame or pain keep you from seeking help.
- You can't fix a relationship that doesn't have a solid foundation.
- When people see that you are working to improve your situation, they will offer some assistance in helping you to reach your goal. But first you must begin to do your part.

CHAPTER 4

A New Beginning: Just the Two of Us

My wish was finally granted, but I was nervous. I had never lived alone, and I missed the security of being around my siblings. Living alone wasn't all it was cracked up to be at first. In order for me to feel secure, I had to identify every sound. I was a nervous wreck unless I could identify why the floors or doors creaked.

Eric and I moved into our own place in late 1971. Being by myself wasn't all fun and games. As much chaos as I had experienced living with so many siblings, there was comfort knowing someone was always there to help or listen when things weren't going well. Our close quarters meant there was never much time to reflect or feel isolated. Our home was filled entirely with alpha-females, so there was never a dull moment. We all had the gift of gab which led to wicked name-calling and all-out brawls.

I should have been as happy as a lark to be an adult in my own space, but that wasn't so in the beginning. There was no one I could laugh my fears away with. There was no one there to tell me that I was being childish or a scaredy-cat. I was responsible for every little thing. I had to remember that I didn't have my mother for direction and guidance, so I learned to plan.

At this point in my life, I hadn't learned how to drive so it took a whole lot of pre-planning to get to the market on the bus schedule. Coming back was really hard. I would be loaded down with groceries and all kinds of things necessary for a toddler. Negotiating before getting into a jitney was a must. Some drivers were decent enough to haul the bags to the porch stoop; however, many of the others refused to help. I learned to always ask the driver if he would help me up the stoop before I accepted the ride.

Grandma Louise had purchased a new car for Gerald, but he never came by to take me grocery shopping or to do any of the things that I would expect him to do as Eric's father. My son and I were truly on our own. Looking back, I just can't believe how absent he was from our lives. He had no real curiosity about taking care of his child. Gerald seemed content just to be able to say that he had a son. This was something that he felt that he could boast about but for which he would not be held accountable. Any clothing or toys that Eric received from his paternal family came mostly from great-grandmother Louise, and those actions were prompted by suggestions from Grandpa Ernest.

Because I had been partially responsible for my youngest siblings, planning wasn't totally foreign to me. I was also never without some type of assistance or guidance. I was able to reach out to my sister Wanda for parenting advice. My oldest sister, Glenda, was the one I could go to for advice on dealing with men—specifically Gerald. She was the eldest of us girls. When I complained to her about how Gerald did not offer to help me at all, Glenda began to explain some things to me.

"As long as you're not going to lie down with him, he's not going to do anything for you or Eric. He's not interested in Eric except for bragging rights. Your relationship has to be on his terms, not yours. Get over it, and start your life over. You made a mistake; you know how you got pregnant so the second time won't be a mistake. Don't deal with him anymore," she said.

I followed Glenda's advice and moved on. I adjusted my attitude and did not behave as if I was a victim. I kept hearing her words: "Don't waste time trying to make him the bad guy. You must move on."

I found work at Spiegel's Warehouse for the Christmas rush. I was a good worker, so they found little projects for me. However, after four months, I was released. Eric and I reverted to our old routine. We would wake up every morning, eat breakfast together, and walk over to Wanda's house to visit. Eric always played with his cousins Randy and Dena. Wanda and I would call them the Three Amigos. They were extremely close growing up. Eric was the typical 1-year-old with high energy. He was fearless. I often tell people he was like the little engine that could. He was small, but he had such a big presence. That presence continued throughout his childhood and adult life.

Gerald Reappears

Sometime after my frank talk with Glenda, Gerald dropped by the apartment unexpectedly. He was in a bad state; it seemed to me that he had been on some sort of binge. I wasn't aware that he had a drug habit. The air was charged with tension, and I felt a wave of dread and nervousness with his presence. When he showed up, it was a muggy evening in the late summer. He spent very little time talking and playing with Eric. At some point he was talking to me in a manner that suggested that he was interested in rekindling our relationship. I cut the conversation short and told him that our relationship was over. During that time, Gerald had visitation rights with his son, and he introduced Eric to several of his female friends. I had the good fortune to know Gerald's father well. Ernest was a wonderful man, but he was one of the most carnal people I had ever met. His needs came first; he didn't care about anything other than satisfying his desires. Nothing got in the way of that. Having spent a great amount of time with Mr. Ernest Mundy, I could see that his second son was cut from the same cloth. Witnessing the emotional destruction Ernest had caused others, I could see that my life with Gerald would unfold in that same manner. Like his father, Gerald was dealing with multiple women. I would experience the same type of betrayal. I would have been a fool to recommence my relationship with him.

Gerald wasn't happy that I rebuffed him. He got mad and made sure to let me know how many women he had and how happy they were to be in his life. At this point, things got heated, and he pushed me up against the wall in the main room of my little studio apartment. Eric had been watching. I quickly said to his father, "Let's go into the kitchen." I didn't want Eric to witness us arguing because at this point I thought we were going to come to blows. Gerald was single-minded, and he was insisting that we sleep together. I told him that we had only one room and that we were not going to do anything of the sort. At this age, Eric was old enough to understand that we were quarreling, and he became fretful. Gerald pushed me back against the wall, and I went directly into fight mode and began resisting him. I suddenly felt compelled to stop tussling and told him, "I'm not going to be with you. If you force me against my will, understand that when I am able, I will call the police and have you arrested for rape." This stopped him in his tracks, and he began hurling insults at me. He couldn't believe that I had refused him and all that he represented. When he paused, I told him, "We are done. You can come see your son, but I have no intention of rekindling our toxic relationship." After that, his visits became random and rare.

During one of these infrequent visits, I told Gerald that I had gone down to the 12th Street police station to file for child support. The courts generally put all the burden of establishing paternity on the mother. In the early 1970s, we didn't have The Jerry Springer Show where women could go on stage and confront the father of their children on national television. No DNA testing was available to shame men into providing support for their children. Gerald's response to my seeking child support was a direct threat. He told me that if I took him to court, he would bring friends to testify that I had slept with them as well. It would be their collective word against mine. He promised me that once he was finished with me in the court of law, I wouldn't get a dime from him. Never would I have expected such a horrible response from him just because I sought financial support for his son.

Gerald had actually acknowledged Eric by signing his birth certificate, so when he threatened to disparage my character to avoid financial responsibility for his son, I was devastated. My heated response was a threat to have him killed. He was a warlord for a notorious gang. At the time he was in jail but was due to get out any day. I told Gerald that if I mentioned to my brother that he was willing to destroy my character in court, he would not live to see another day. My brother or one of his fellow gang members would have taken care of him. I was devastated by his vicious threats and the fact that he would publicly accuse me of such a horrendous act just to avoid paying child support. After I calmed down, I realized his words had allowed me to further see his true character. I just couldn't believe that he could come up with such a rotten thing to say just off the top of his head to avoid responsibility. Needless to say, however, his words shut me down. Dealing with my teen pregnancy and my forfeiting an opportunity to go to college because I had decided to keep my baby was humiliating enough—and now this ploy! I felt physical pain as if he had stabbed me in the heart. I closed my mouth and decided that it wasn't worth taking this fool to court. Doing so would have only led to more shame and sorrow. When it came to Gerald, I was truly on my own. I reflected on what he had so callously said and thought to myself, "He's not worth the pain and effort of fighting in court for any child support the court would force him to pay." A couple years later, however, his mean-spirited words and threats would come back to haunt him.

Dealing with Gerald's pushback and antics were really reality checks for me. I realized that for any money Eric and I needed, I would have to earn it. I put it out of my mind that I would find the perfect job right away. I recalled my great-grandmother's words to my uncles whenever they complained about not finding employment: "A piece of job is better than nothing." Keeping her words in mind kept me humble as I would only find temporary and seasonal jobs for almost 2 years. However, I carried on, declaring that I was not a victim. I continued to follow Glenda's sage advice. Trying to make Gerald the bad guy was a waste of time and energy. Only he could decide how he would respond to fatherhood. I just had to listen to those who offered me wise advice and guidance.

Even now as I look back, I'm grateful that I was able to experience many acts of kindness toward my son and me. I am even grateful for my trials which made me wiser and stronger. I still had my little village: my stepmother who made sure my dad looked out for us, kind neighbors, and the two teachers who stayed in touch with me after my graduation. Later, I will tell you about an imminent tragedy that was averted and about how listening to a still voice possibly saved both my life and Eric's life as well.

I finally got my first full-time job offer from one of the largest employers in the city, The United States Postal Service. I took their test and qualified for a mail carrier position in Blue Island, Illinois. However, I had a small problem. I still didn't have my driver's license. I had expected to get a mail sorter position at the downtown location because I knew I could catch the El or the bus there. I had to decline the offer.

Mother 2 Mother: A New Beginning: Just the Two of Us

Wow, Eric and I had come a mighty long way! I will not lie. Getting to the point of relative independence did not come without setbacks. What got us through was my ability to not look back too long on the anger and bitterness from my relationship with Eric's biological father. Whenever I wallowed in my misery and disappointments, I became stuck. I couldn't stop thinking about why he left his son. I learned to use those negative thoughts as fuel to make a liar out of those who said that I had ruined my chances of having a better life by keeping my baby.

Maybe your story isn't about a pregnancy, but these words will serve as a template for you to get unstuck from any bad situation that comes your way.

LESSONS LEARNED

- Don't let loneliness allow you to stay in dead-end relationships.
- You are stronger than you think. Look back and activate those skills you used when you were helping your siblings or younger relatives.
- Yes, you will struggle, but having a solid plan will reduce a lot of your stress.
- Surround yourself with people who want to see you prosper.
- Reduce the time spent around negative friends and relatives. They will hinder you from moving into a better headspace.

CHAPTER 5

A Night I'll Never Forget

One late winter evening Eric's breath was unusually shallow, and he began to wheeze. I noticed he caught a cold the night before, and I used my mom's tried and true home remedy to try and get a handle on it. My mama used Vicks vapor rub for everything, and so did I. I greased Eric up with Vicks and put a dab of it in his mouth along with a bit of Father John cough syrup. I remembered how my mom kept a kettle on the back jet to add some moisture in the air, so I also boiled a pot of water to increase the humidity in the apartment. I was hoping his cold wouldn't get any worse, but it did. I called my sister Wanda, and she told me that I should start to check his temperature. Each time I checked it I realized it was slowly creeping up! She was unable to get her husband to take off to drive us to the hospital. She didn't have a car.

His little belly rose up and down with each weak breath, and I began to panic. I called for a cab. The first cab company said they were sending a driver for us. After an hour passed I called back, and they lied and said that someone was on their way. Finally, one of the operators told me none of the drivers would come to my area because of the gang fights and violence. I started to call around to the other cab companies. I was begging for help to get my son to the hospital. I could see that his condition was deteriorating.

At this time, Gerald's visits were rare; we didn't even speak much over the phone. However, that changed the night Eric was really sick. I was in desperate need of Gerald's help to get us to the emergency room. I called around, frantically trying to track him down. I couldn't reach him through his father or either of his great-grandmothers. I finally called Eric's grandmother; maybe she knew how to contact him. She answered the phone and promised to try to call around to let Gerald know that his son was sick.

After a long nerve racking wait, Gerald reached out to me. He had promised me that he'd come get us. I pleaded for him to hurry. I waited for a long time, but no blowing horn signaled his arrival. At some point, I realized that he was not coming! I accepted that I would have to walk over to South Parkway to hail a jitney cab or take the No. 1 bus to get Eric the medical attention he desperately needed. I was frightened out of my mind because I knew how dangerous it was for us to be out at 2:00 a.m. My fears had further delayed getting my baby much-needed medical help.

Eric's fever continued to climb, and his breathing became labored. He was still a toddler at the time. He began to wheeze and cough until he gagged so I knew I had to do the unthinkable. We had to go outside to get him help. During this time in Chicago, unless you were affiliated with one of the gangs, you were at risk of being targeted. They didn't care if you were a woman with a child or not. It was way too dangerous to be out and about at 2:00 a.m. so I was torn between seeking care for my son and exposing him to the dangers awaiting us outside. In our town, only predators roamed at night looking for prey. Whatever was happening to Eric at this point was my fault because I didn't act sooner. We had to take our chances and make our way to the hospital, alone and without Gerald.

I dressed us both for the long, cold walk. I quietly opened our apartment door and shut the light off in the vestibule. I locked up my apartment in the dark. I was blindly seeking the keyhole. We eased down the stoop and then the sidewalk. Eric was holding on to me tightly as he whimpered and wheezed. I shushed him so that I could listen for trouble. Thankfully, it was bitter cold, and not many people would venture out in the blustery, freezing weather. We didn't need any unwanted attention. We made it down another block and then two more until we reached South Parkway safely. The snow had a hard crust on it. It had to be below freezing. I silently prayed and was grateful for the frigid weather as it would keep many indoors. I listened for footfalls that didn't match mine. Soon enough, ever so slightly, I heard another set of steps! I walked faster in the snow tracks; all the while, the stalker kept pace with us ever so quietly! I could barely make out the faint sounds of his footfalls. Chills ran up my spine! Whoever was following us didn't wish to be detected. I prepared for the imminent confrontation! Was it a gangbanger? Was this the night the gang would make good on their promise to finish us off? Was this the night they would get the revenge they promised? The night was dark. There was no moonlight. It was just a dark sky filled with swirling various shades of darker storm clouds. Only the waist-high snowdrifts and the weak lights glowing through the vestibule door panels lit our path. Suddenly, I realized that the quiet footfalls were almost upon us. My brain screamed, "He's too close!

Danger! React now!"

I effortlessly tossed my son onto a mound of packed snow and whirled toward the approaching figure. It was a tall stranger. I told him to get away from me. He replied quietly, "I don't mean you no harm." I was more angry than afraid at this point and was poised to fight for our lives.

I said, "You must mean us no good. Why are you creeping behind us? I want you to leave us alone. My son is sick, and I just need to get him to the hospital. "Quickly, he lurched toward me and pulled me toward him! I was beyond shock. Didn't he see me as I tossed my young son onto a snow bank? I screamed angry, harsh words. I told him that I didn't want to be bothered and that I was trying to get my child to the emergency room.

"Get away from us!" I yelled. The stranger just kept up his calm one-sided conversation as I tried to wrestle myself out of his grip. I finally slipped away from his hold and began to fight earnestly for my child's safety and mine. He'd seen me with a baby. "He's crazy," I thought. No one sane would act this way.

As we continued our struggle, a car slowly came to a halt behind my attacker's back! It was a jitney cab! Oh my God, I couldn't believe it! Jitney cabs couldn't operate off their South Parkway route. They could drop customers off, but they couldn't pick up a fare on that route.

The cab driver tooted his horn to attract our attention. He leaned over to roll down the side window and asked, "Miss, are you alright?"

I screamed, "NO! I don't know this guy. He's attacking me! I need help getting to Michael Reese Hospital. My son is very sick!"

The cabbie had his gun on the front passenger seat. He leveled it at my attacker and told me, "Pick up that damn baby and get in the back seat." The cab driver never raised his voice and kept the gun leveled at my attacker. As we drove away, a frightful thought filled my head for a second. Had I done the right thing in getting into this cab with the stranger with a gun? Was my situation with the stranger without a gun the lesser of the two evils? As we drove away, the cabbie asked, "Were you harmed in any way, Miss?" Such kindness from a complete stranger made me burst into tears. I thought to myself that my son's father gave us no such thought.

The cab driver drove us straight to the hospital and gave me his number on a slip of paper just in case I needed a ride home. He was indeed an angel sent from heaven!

Eric's condition seemed to have gotten worse during my scary ordeal of having to toss him in the snow bank. The cabbie escorted me into the emergency room. He told the attending nurse what had happened. She asked if I needed medical attention. I said that I was okay, and I refused it. She then quickly checked Eric in, and we were rushed to a bed for his examination. Eric's diagnosis was severe bronchitis and diarrhea. He would need to be kept for at least twenty-four hours. I was not letting my baby out of my sight after the ordeal we had just undergone. I cried and refused to let him be taken from me. "Okay," the doctor finally said. He gave in to my pleas and agreed to give me twenty-four hours to get the diarrhea under control. He warned me to keep to the medication schedule and to return if Eric's condition did not improve. He promised that he would contact protective services if he did not hear back from me within the specified time frame. As he pulled out his prescription pad, I told him that I couldn't get to a drugstore. He nodded his head and stepped away. When he came back, he had brought back enough free samples to treat Eric's bronchial infection and asked if I had white rice at home. I wondered why he asked such a strange question, but I nodded yes. He proceeded to write instructions for making a homemade concoction to stop Eric's diarrhea. I had to boil rice until it created a starchy milky white liquid. I was to give it to my son every two hours with a bit of Karo syrup. He asked for my phone number and warned me that if things weren't under control in twenty-four hours I would have to return so that Eric could get proper care in the hospital. The doctor told me that my son would die if I didn't do as instructed because of the severity of the diarrhea. I often wondered whether Eric's doctor had learned this folk remedy as a Peace Corps doctor. Eric drank so much rice water then that it's a miracle that he will even eat rice now! That remedy worked, and my son steadily recovered.

Moving on Up! Finding Steady Work

In early 1972, on a lark, I found full-time employment at Argonne National Laboratory. That would not have happened if I had not graduated from high school with a certificate in printing. The opportunity came about one day when I was in my former high school neighborhood for a routine clinic appointment. I felt a wave of nostalgia and a strong desire to stop by the school for a visit. As I walked through the long entryway, lost in my bittersweet memories, I heard someone call my name, "Miss Craig! Miss Craig!" It was my old counselor, Mr. Chapman. He eagerly told me that Argonne National Laboratory was hiring. Dunbar was a feeder school for many of the skilled trades Argonne needed. They had inquired for female applicants to fill a position as a Lithographer in their pre-press department. He thought of me, as I was one of a few female students who had completed the printing apprenticeship. He mentioned that he had called my home several times, but our phone number on record was no longer in service. I was ecstatic, and I just couldn't believe my good fortune! He mentioned that the position was still available because Argonne was only looking to hire a female for that position because of EEOC mandates.

After I saw the address, I said, "But, sir, that's out in Downers Grove. I've never learned how to drive."

He asked quickly, "Do you know Sylvester Reid?"

Of course I did! Sylvester and I had lived in the same apartment complex on 45th and Vincennes, and we had been friends since we were in the fifth grade. "Well, we got him a job there as well, and I happen to have his number," Mr. Chapman explained. I'm sure that I did a happy dance right in the middle of his little office. I called Sylvester—and then, of course, Wanda, my rock—right there from the counselor's office.

I could not contain myself as I told Wanda that I needed her to convince Jimmy to drive me to my interview. She convinced him to take me. Mr. Chapman arranged for the interview around

Jimmy's schedule. I got the job! Sylvester and I worked out the driving arrangements, and he promised to swing by my apartment before we headed to work so I could first drop Eric off at his auntie's house.

I had my first full-time, permanent job! I hired Wanda as Eric's full-time paid babysitter. I was finally able to do something nice to pay her back for all her help and support. Working for the federal government provided me with a solid salary, medical insurance, and great benefits. I set a firm goal and date to get off the welfare rolls. After eight months on the job, I called my case worker and told him I no longer needed their services. He asked me to come into the office, so he could review my file and determine if I could still qualify for some benefits. He told me to bring in my pay stub, current bills, and rental agreement so he could go over everything and determine for sure whether my benefits should be reduced or if my case truly needed to be closed. I told him, "No, I'm getting off welfare." I appreciated the help, but I didn't need it anymore.

I had one request before closing my file. I told him we needed to get a new washing machine and a new mattress. Back in the day, you were generally given a voucher for used appliances and mattresses. I heard him chuckle over the phone, and he said, "You got a lot of nerve making demands!"

I said, "I'm not making demands. I am trying to get on my feet and getting a new machine and mattress would really help." I had shown him my determination to find a better life for my son and myself by finding work and taking myself off the welfare roll. He laughed and told me to come in to pick up the requested vouchers for the new items. He said that they could be redeemed at Polk Brothers Furniture Store. I didn't believe for a minute I was being unreasonable. I had taken full responsibility for making a better life for Eric. Our better future rested on the decisions I would have to make.

Our lives improved with my better-paying job. I was finally able to move from the studio apartment into a two-bedroom apartment and finally get Eric out of his crib. He was climbing out of it anyway! The vouchers were part of my plan to improve our station in life. I know it sounds silly, but after I got the appliances, I was over the moon. No used furniture for us! I was too young to get a line of credit, so I put my first bedroom suite on layaway. I also started my first savings plan through my job. All federal employees were encouraged to purchase savings bonds, and I got on the automatic plan right away. I had been used to living on a tight budget, and I didn't go overboard with non-essential purchases because of my higher wages. I would continue to buy savings bonds throughout my career. I bought them for my grandchildren as well.

During this period of my life, I kissed a few frogs. However, like they say, when you know better, you must do better. When I encountered behaviors or traits I didn't want in a relationship, I didn't waste any time ending those relationships.

LESSONS LEARNED

- I realized before it was too late that I acted in my feelings/emotions! While I understood the seriousness of Eric's condition, his father didn't truly have a clue. He dismissed my plea.
- You gotta know when to hold them and when to fold them. You gotta know when to walk away and when to run!
- We must learn to operate in the truth. Making everything personal allows logic to fly out of the window.
- Pay attention to those who are a part of your life and your child's life. Being unaware can create serious consequences.
- Create a life plan. Write it down, and have a timeline for your milestones to be completed.
- Have everything in place so you can move quickly when an opportunity opens up.
- Stay ready by gaining new skills if needed. Be prepared for great things to happen.
- As your pay increases. Start setting aside a little money each payday; it will be the single most important thing you'll need to start improving your lifestyle.

CHAPTER 6

Meeting My Mate

In late 1972, I met my husband, Jesse, through his friendship with my Uncle David.

Jesse was somewhat of an introvert, so he didn't have much to say during our first encounter. Over the upcoming New Year's holiday, Jesse came back to town, and we happened to be at the same party. Afterward, we had a long conversation, and he convinced David to invite me and two of my sisters to Detroit for a visit. At the end of our visit, he asked if he could come to Chicago to see me again. I was attracted to him on several levels, but what pleased me the most was the fact that he did not try to win my heart through my son. Jesse was truly kind to Eric during his visits, but he never came bearing gifts; I liked that about him. I was convinced that he had honorable intentions. After more visits to Chicago, Jesse told me that my personality and mouth were so big that he didn't know if he stood a chance with me but that he was glad he had followed through and asked me for that first official date.

When we officially became a couple, he went to his mom and asked her what she thought of me. She said that she liked my sister Wanda! I had first met his mom when I visited Detroit with several of my sisters. Jesse quickly cleared up the confusion and told his mom that Wanda was already married, and he described me again. She was lukewarm about us dating because I had a child. I was also somewhat leery of developing a relationship because of my son. I didn't want to enter into a relationship that I didn't believe would allow us to go from two to a family.

We moved forward cautiously. Jesse visited us in the middle and at the end of each month because of his pay schedule. Slowly, he bonded with Eric. Jesse took my son to his friend's barber and got him his first haircut. Eric had a ponytail at the time, and Jesse insisted that I cut it. Jesse used his biweekly visits to make time for the two of us. His interactions with Eric were always pleasant, and they got along great.

A year into our courtship, he flew me up to Detroit for a visit. He proposed during a road trip to Toronto. Jesse said he was interested in settling down and creating a family with me and Eric. When his mother first heard that Jesse had asked me to marry him, she was not happy. She felt that he could find someone better. At the time, Jesse was one of the first in his family to graduate from college. She told him that taking on a ready-made family was not wise. He countered that he and I were a great fit. Once she realized that Jesse had made up his mind, she embraced us. After our marriage, Grandma Shirley (Jesse's mom) did a great job of babysitting her "grandson" long before we grew our family.

Jesse and I were engaged for a year. He wanted to save some money and find a place for us to live. We decided on a date one year later. Jesse wanted us to move to Detroit and begin our new life with him there. My ideal plan was to remain in Chicago. A final decision had to be made. Where would it be? Would we start our life as a family in Detroit or Chicago? Trying to decide which city offered the best opportunities was hard on both of us.

In the beginning, I felt that it would have been best for Jesse to relocate to Chicago. He was a logistics specialist with General Motors, and they had a berth at O'Hare Airport. It would have been a perfect fit for him—or so I thought. But that wasn't something that he even wanted to entertain. It wasn't that he would be leaving his hometown. After high school, he played basketball at Texas Southern University, so the idea of leaving Detroit wasn't the issue; he just felt that we had a better chance of growing and owning a home in Detroit. Of course, I wanted to remain in the place I called home, even though I was actually born in the D, and I had an extended family there!

I was still working at Argonne, and there was potential for growth if I remained there. Back and forth we went. I tried to show him all the perks of living in Chicago. Jesse was not interested in that bustling city. He was adamant that Detroit had a lot more to offer. We negotiated back and forth all during our engagement, but needless to say, Detroit won the contest.

Mother 2 Mother: Meeting My Mate

There was a missed opportunity to connect with Gerald about my possible marriage. I remained in regular contact with both Eric's paternal grand and great-grandmothers. My sharing such a major life change with them did not impact their keeping Gerald's current drug usage a secret. Had there been honest dialogue, Gerald, Eric and I could have had a different experience. I shared Jesse's desire to make us a family since Gerald was totally absent from his son's life long before I met my future husband. Still they covered up for him. After my marriage, I sent many registered letters to Grandma Mundy concerning Eric's pending adoption. Whenever I followed up, she simply said that Gerald was aware that she signed for receipt of my registered letters regarding our request for Eric's legal adoption. Gerald never reached out to me to state that he would relinquish his rights, so we could proceed. Nor did he protest about my multiple requests to have our son's name legally changed to Thomas. Grandma Gwen never stopped accepting the court notices, but I would never know whether or not Gerald read them. It was ironic that their desire to protect Gerald at such a high price yet stay connected with Eric would later cause unspeakable damage to both him and our entire family.

LESSONS LEARNED

- Enabling someone is not love, and it hinders his or her growth.
- My first assumption about Gerald's inability to be a part of his son's life was flawed because it was based on information his family shared or withheld.
- Withholding the truth is sometimes painful, but it must be spoken in order to build healthy relationships.
- Engaging in honest conversation is necessary in order to reach a sound conclusion.

PART II

IN THE SECRET

"Don't betray your progression by running
back to the ones you've outgrown."
— *Unknown*

CHAPTER 7

The Move to Detroit

Jesse came up a few days before we were to be married and asked why I had not begun to pack or clear out my apartment. Being a practical woman, I had not actually resigned from my job nor had I cancelled the lease on my apartment. I had a kid to raise, and I wasn't about to jump the gun and quit my job before I was actually legally married. I had not experienced a relationship with a man whose word was his bond, so I was playing it safe. I had accrued two weeks of vacation time, so my plan was to use it as my two-week notice of resignation.

Jesse and I went downtown and scheduled a civil marriage ceremony with the Chicago Department Justice of Peace. For my special day, I called my mom earlier in our engagement to share my good news and ask for her presence to witness my marriage! She had left Chicago a few years earlier, moved back to Detroit, and reunited with my stepfather. She did not come back. However, sweet Wanda gladly acted in her stead. My Uncle David stood in as Jesse's best man. Afterwards, we all stopped at the Berghoff for lunch and a celebratory drink.

I approached my manager the day after our nuptials, and I told him that I had just gotten married and that I was moving to Detroit. I always worked hard to maintain great relationships so while my manager was not happy with the approach, he understood the reason why I waited for the last minute to announce my leaving the job. He wished me good luck, as he was aware of my struggles as a single parent. After our talk, I felt confident asking him to write me a letter of reference in case I found work in Detroit. That reference letter would later help me during my interview for National Reproductions and subsequently allow me to beat out two other applicants. Over the next few days we prepared for our move. We both were so happy to begin our new life. Jesse then said to me, "I was tired of driving up to Chi-town twice a month! I want our family to be together in one place."

My oldest sister Glenda, her husband JB, and several of my work buddies came by to help us pack and load Eric's and my belongings into a U-Haul truck. Leaving the place that I called home was bittersweet, yet I was over the moon to have found a good man who not only loved me but also wanted to be a father to my child. It was almost too good to be true. How could I be so lucky as to be introduced to someone who was so open-minded that the idea of raising someone else's child didn't seem foreign to him? I was very much in love, but as a single mom, I was also concerned. I had to make sure that the man with whom I planned on spending the rest of my life with would be compatible with my son. During our courtship, Jesse had shown that he was a good man. We initially started off as friends and later fell in love. Jesse was certain that he wanted children, which was good news, as I already had a child! He wanted three to be exact; I, on the other hand, was content with my one. We agreed during our engagement that we would have two more children after we had bonded as a new family.

Nonetheless, Jesse was very sensitive to my feelings. He also knew that Eric's biological father was absent. He declared that he would adopt Eric and make him a Thomas.

I still hadn't reached out to Gerald concerning Jesse, yet I introduced Jesse to several of Eric's paternal relatives. By this time, Gerald was totally out of the picture as far as his son was concerned. Gerald had to be aware of my pending marriage because Jesse had met both Eric's grandmother and great-grandmother during our courtship. I am certain that Gerald had been told of my pending marriage, but he never reached out to inquire how my marriage would affect his stake in his son's life. He never inquired about whether we would be staying in a local area or far away. He never inquired about how he might be able to get in touch with us afterwards. The two men actually never met until Gerald visited Detroit with the mother of one of his other sons. By then, Eric was probably ten or older.

Our Move to Detroit for a New Life
With the help of my new mother-in-law, we found housing in a flat near Hamtramck on a little street called Burnside. Our transition went rather smoothly. I brought a lot of my furnishings from my apartment to our new place, so we did not need much to set up. Jesse's mom hosted a small family gathering to introduce me to his extended family. For the most part, it went without too much drama. My family had returned to Detroit before I got married, so they were settled in. I still had five of my younger sisters living at home, as well as my youngest brother. While Wanda and her family closed any gaps concerning family involvements after my mother's move, my youngest siblings picked up where they left off before their move back to Detroit. Eric only sparingly saw the paternal side of his family, so he didn't appear to experience any emotional shock when we left Chicago. I don't believe he experienced a deep sense of disconnection because my extended family gathered him right back up into the fold. Soon after we settled into married life, Jesse found a lawyer and asked him to begin the adoption process. We were told that we must be married one year before we could petition the court for adoption. I reached out to Gerald via his mother at this point to make him aware of our pending adoption request. His threats to slander my character in

court to avoid child support had come back to bite him in his butt. He would now need to come to Michigan to appear in court to establish his paternal rights and to either reject or agree to our appeal for adoption.

We continued living on Burnside, and it became apparent that a few families on our block would cause us problems. We had not been there two months when one of the neighbors came knocking on our door after Jesse left for work. It was an attempt to befriend me. Of course, she was always borrowing things. First, it was a cup of sugar or some potatoes. After she noticed that Jesse smoked, she started asking for a few cigarettes. I told her that I didn't lend out what wasn't mine and to please come back later and ask my husband. Finally, her requests began to involve borrowing money. I began to distance myself from her and the other neighbors.

Several of the kids were forceful as well, and they would take over Eric's toys when he brought them out to play. They were not like his cousins or the neighborhood kids with whom Eric was accustomed to playing with in Chicago. He was a social kid, and he wanted to fit in. The one toy that was his pride and joy was his Big Wheel, a sweet lime-green tricycle model that his granddad Ernest had bought him before we moved to Detroit. He had decked it out with multi-colored streamers flying from the handlebars and had added something on the spokes that made a racket. Eric willingly shared this special toy with the kids on the block. A couple of older boys later took the Big Wheel from Eric after he allowed them to ride it. He came into the house crying, and he was very upset. Being the tiger mother that I was, old lessons I had learned flooded my head. I could not believe that I was responding to that situation just like my mom. Jesse wasn't home, but I sent my son back outside and told him to get the Big Wheel back! I didn't care how; he just needed to get it back. I didn't really expect Eric to encounter real problems retrieving it! I assumed that most parents thought like me; my son was never allowed to bring things home that he "found."

However, that was not the way they operated on Burnside; it was a "finders-keepers" mentality over there! Or not exactly finders-keeper—more like if you came across someone whom you felt was weak, their property was up for the taking. In the end, Eric somehow found a pop bottle, broke off the bottom of it and threatened the boys with bodily harm if they didn't give him back his scooter. They were a little older, but Eric always had the heart of a lion. He basically told them, "You know, somebody's going to get cut or hurt. My mama said that I had to come back with my Big Wheel." He successfully retrieved the Big Wheel. One of the mothers came knocking at our door, and she was complaining that Eric had been threatening her son. I told her that he was told to retrieve his stuff, and that was that. She got my message; I needed them to see that we were not easy prey! After realizing what type of parents lived on the block, I always made sure that either Jesse or I were outside when Eric was riding, and we never left his toys outside overnight.

I soon began to be bored with being a housewife. Getting a modest allowance was a grind after having earned enough money to enjoy some discretionary spending. I scoured the Sunday paper looking for another job in the printing industry. I was determined to find work even though my husband said many times that he didn't want me to work. Without any leads in the employment ads, I turned my search to the Yellow Pages. After calling and interviewing at several places, I was asked to come to National Reproduction one Saturday for four hours without pay; the manager wanted to see if I had the skills to run his prepress department. I was hired as a litho-camera operator and platemaker after just two hours. During my employment there, I befriended Mike Ivan. He was laid off from Ford Motor Company at the time. Our friendship led to my employment at Ford. Mike had promised to get me a position there when he was called back. I was skeptical as I had made many attempts to gain employment there without any success. Again, by building a healthy relationship with my coworker without seeking anything in return, he opened doors at Ford Motor Company for me.

I enrolled in college for the first time at the Society of Arts and Crafts. I worked toward a fine arts degree, yet I still had no desire to drive. Jesse was working a swing shift at GM, so depending on his shift, he either babysat Eric and dropped me off at work or took us to the bus stop on his day shift rotation. During this period, my mom babysat for us. Eric and I took a bus to my mom's house. I was always cordial with the driver so at some point he asked where I was going. I told him that Eric and I rode two buses to get to my mom and that I rushed to get back to the route before my transfer expired. He quickly worked out a deal and punched my transfer for a later time. This allowed me to use my transfer after the time limit so that I could save the cost of a daily fare. The last bus took me downtown to work. A new friend in college introduced us to Mrs. McLaughlin. Through her, we experienced the joy of leasing a home. We moved from Burnside Street. We were now close to my mom's place and Eric's school. Our new home was located on Atkinson, close to the storied Boston-Edison area. We celebrated our second year of marriage there.

After the one-year period, we began the adoption process. We were instructed to send all communications via registered mail to prove that we were acting in good faith towards the biological parent. During this time, I received a call from Gerald's mom; her daughter would be in Detroit. She was a cheerleader, and her college was playing in a tournament against the University of Detroit. She wanted to know if it was okay to stop by and see her nephew. Jesse was okay with it, so I gave her our address. I could not have foreseen that my kind gesture would morph into a series of dialogues with Eric's paternal side that would shake my family to its core.

Before I got married, Gerald's family knew that my relationship with him was dead. More importantly, they were well aware of his lifestyle and how he interacted with Eric. The women carried the family banner and wanted to claim Eric as part of their clan. Unfortunately, I was naïve. Their claiming Eric meant that they would work to undermine his ability to bond with Jesse.

From the onset of my marriage, we included Gerald's family in our lives. Grandma Gwen became a frequent, welcomed guest. She came for holidays and sometimes just for a getaway. She had close family in Detroit, yet she always found her way to the Thomas's home where we treated her with the utmost kindness. She was so well-treated that her visits continued. Her visits began first in our rented apartment, and they have continued over the span of thirty-plus years.

Boy, I had made so much progress! I was in a good marriage. My son was thriving, and I had a good relationship with my mom. As the eldest sibling in Detroit, I made sure that we included my sisters and brother whenever we took Eric on outings.

My only real challenge was that my husband felt irritated when he had to drive me to the places in which only I was interested, like the mall. Whenever he took me shopping, he set a time for how long he was going to be stuck in the mall. After one particular heated argument about his having to cart me everywhere I wanted to go, Jesse said, "It's time you learned how to drive." On his next day off, he came home with a brand new '76 Cutlass Supreme. He handed me the keys and said, "I'm tired of driving you around. Go get your driver's license." I didn't have my driving permit or a lesson plan. But, ready or not, he started to teach me how to drive!

He was not a patient teacher. After one hard drive around Belle Isle, I jumped out of my car, leaving the car door open and the engine running. I had enough, and I demanded that he help me find somebody else to teach me how to drive. It took me a long time before I was ready to take my road test. After the examiner and I got into my car, he turned and looked at me and asked, "Who would allow you to drive their new car and you don't even have your license yet?" He was stunned when I told him that my husband bought it for me. I did pretty good during the driving part of the test, but, for the life of me, I could not pass the parallel parking portion. My DMV examiner must have felt sorry for me since I already had a car because I kept knocking the barriers down. Frustrated, he told me to drive around the block and just pull in the first empty slot in front of the DMV. I think he passed me because I already had a car. My cousin, Luella, had used my car to take her youngest brother Tony for his road test earlier at another location. After I got my temporary license, she said, "I'm driving you both home, but I'm stopping at the liquor store first. I need a drink to calm my nerves." I bought her a pint of Bacardi Rum.

Jesse was relieved that we no longer had to walk to the bus stop, especially during the winter when the night time came earlier. He always said that my chances of getting a better job increased because many of the printing companies were outside of the city, and suburban bus service was not reliable. Was he ever right! Within ninety days of my getting my driver's license, Mike made good on his promise to me; he put in a good word at Ford Motor Company, and they actually called me at my current job and offered me a position as a Microfilm tech. This would be the first time that I drove myself to an interview. I was fortunate to work for Ford Motor Company for almost thirty-one uninterrupted years. That's when I learned how good relationships could open doors you could not open yourself.

Of course, Jesse tagged along, as I had never driven outside the city. I was now twenty-four years old. When our lease was up on Atkinson, Jesse decided that we were not going to renew it. We both had great jobs; he said that it was time that we bought our first home. Later on, when our family grew, Grandma Gwen continued to visit us, but she favored Eric over his sisters. However, it was never at a level that caused tension because our children's relationships were healthy, so I shrugged it off as something that the Mundy women did. Love your males no matter what, and raise the girls! Grandma Gwen expressed her deep disappointment over the way we handled certain situations. She expressed how often she had cried over our parenting style, such as how we made our son walk to middle school in the cold and snowy winters of Detroit. She would cry that sad refrain for years until I finally had enough of her condemnation of the way we had treated our son. To her, he was a prince who should have only gotten the best of whatever Jesse and I had to offer without any training, chores, or responsibilities. So finally, I calmly asked her, "Do you not recall that his little sister Neco had to walk that same path to the school with him? The distance was too short, so we didn't qualify for the school bus pickup. Did you ever think about how it must have felt to her, walking along with her brother and the other kids on Braile Street, and she was only five years old?"

Grandma was shocked that I would even bring the matter up, and she simply said, "I never thought about her." Mind you, she visited during the winter months and saw the scene play out in front of her eyes. It would be years before I uncovered the depths of Gerald's family's displaced loyalty to Eric. As Eric got older, their betrayal was uncovered bit by bit, and it played a pivotal role in the destruction of our family. My daughters, Eric's sisters, didn't mean a hill of beans to them. They weren't a part of their brood, and they were just girls.

LESSONS LEARNED

- Remember that starting over includes bringing your past along for the ride.
- Be the narrator of your life's story.
- Don't give others the right to tell your truths.

CHAPTER 8

Jesse Brings Up Adoption

Jesse wanted all of our children to share a common last name. I expressed that I did not want more children because they'd have a different last name. My siblings and I had several different last names, and I was always uncomfortable with people saying that we were half-sisters and half-brothers. Our oldest sister, Glenda, would always say in response to those remarks, "When you come out of the same hole, you all are whole brothers and sisters."

Adoption never crossed my mind until Jesse suggested it, and I was very happy that he did so. I never spoke of this to Jesse, but I was overjoyed that he pursued it. This was my own personal hangup. Being one of fourteen children where there were multiple fathers caused a lot of rejection from the various sets of fathers involved, as well as distant estranged family members! I understand my bias. Just because a family is blended, it doesn't mean it's necessary to alter all the children's names to match up with that of the parents. For me, however, it was a Godsend!

The process began in the spring of 1975. Eric was 4 years old. Gerald never acknowledged paternity or filed an appeal against our request for adoption. He simply refused to respond to the registered summons from the courts. The adoption process was held up as we all waited for Gerald to claim paternity and work out whatever came with finally legally acknowledging his son.

A full year passed without any progress in the case. Eric was ready to start kindergarten. I reached out to Gerald's mother again as I had been doing for an entire year. I asked if Gerald had gotten my registered letters. She said that he hadn't come by the house for it. She promised to pass on my message to him. I threatened him, saying that I was going to come to Illinois and establish residency and that I would force his hand in court. I told her that I would petition the courts for five years of back child support. He would be accountable one way or another. Jesse would not continue to be a father and shape his son into a man he would become one day with Gerald getting the honor to say, "My son is a Mundy." I told my husband that there would be another delay. He never got upset nor did he express his opinion on the way Gerald was reacting or shall I say not reacting regarding my request.

I finally got in touch with Gerald and the conversation didn't go well. During our conversation, I asked Gerald what the holdup was in signing off on the adoption. His reply was, "How dare you change my son's last name?" I reminded him that he had never done anything of value for Eric. "Everything that Eric has ever gotten was from your family," I told him. "Your grandparents were the ones who took our son and cared for him. You never actually did anything for him. Remember, you were willing to go to the courthouse to deny him and to slander my character to avoid paying child support if I forced you to court," I added.

That conversation didn't spark anything in Gerald, and I became fed up.

LESSONS LEARNED

- Don't cry over spilled milk. Most of our hardships are blessings in disguise.
- God's plan is always the better plan. My son commented years later that God selected Gerald to give his seed, but God selected Jesse to raise him so that he can become the man that he is today.

CHAPTER 9

Eric Mundy to Eric Thomas

did some research and found out where Gerald worked. I was so angry that I took off, unbeknownst to my husband, and drove to Chicago—and boy, was I ready for battle! He wasn't there that day; he had called off. I was so wound up and frustrated that I was almost in tears.

I was boiling mad and could not go to my sister's house in my present state, so I sought out Grandma Cleo's advice. She just lived a few blocks from the Shell station where Gerald worked. Grandma Cleo was straight as an arrow. She saw life as black-and-white. She loved you to death, but that didn't stop her from seeing your flaws and calling you out. I drove up without calling to announce my visit—it was like that between us. I was a part of her clan. I had earned her respect and her loyalty over the years. She opened the screen door when she saw me approaching. Before I made it through the door, she saw that I was in a rage. She had witnessed the fight her grandson and I had in the years before. She knew what my temper looked like, and she knew about the storm that would result from it! However, Big Cleo was my partner in crime. I knew from our history that she would help me clean up the mess. She never asked me one question.

She went straight to the cupboard and got out her tin coffee can. She was preparing to make us coffee. Now, Grandma Cleo's coffee was old school. She put the grounds in the little basket, filled the percolator with water, turned on the jet, and set the percolator on to brew us a cup or two. She must have known that I would be there awhile. That day, as she tried to calm me down, our coffee steeped until it was almost sludge.

She kept our conversation light as she asked about her first great-grandson, Master Eric, as she always addressed him. She asked about my mom as well. Anything to defuse my agitated disposition. I finally relaxed and told her what had happened and how frustrated I was that Gerald was being so resistant. I just couldn't understand why he would continue to ignore the situation. Big Grandma Cleo talked some sense into me. She said, "Let me handle this." She took care of things. Big Cleo first had a talk with her daughter. She told her that we were good people and that we were in a good place and that everybody needed to settle down and respect that. She said that we were in a happy place and that I wasn't bitter or angry. She explained to them that I had the good sense to realize that Eric and I would not be in Gerald's future and neither would he be in ours.

Whatever she said, it did the trick. The adoption process began without further delays. Big Cleo worked it out. She spoke to Gerald and told him that he was not doing anything for his son and that he was not in a position to do anything for him. She told him that he needed to sign those papers.

Eric was getting ready to begin kindergarten and was still legally a Mundy. Although the process was progressing, it was not completed. I petitioned the Court to have a letter drafted so that

Eric would start school as a Thomas. The judge agreed to grant my request to allow Eric to use the Thomas surname. He was kind enough to write an official court document that allowed Eric to start kindergarten using his new surname of Thomas, even though the process had not yet been finalized.

It eventually all worked itself out in the court system. Eric was finally adopted by default because I had proof that I had done everything in my power to communicate with his father to amicably resolve the adoption. This process took almost two years to complete, and Eric was about 6 years old at this time.

I did not change my son's name out of spite. Many of our friends had children before they married, but Jesse was the only one we knew who actually adopted his wife's child. From my point of view, Jessie managed to hit the proper level of involvement, not too little and not too much. For a change, it all worked in my favor. He spoke of adoption because he truly understood that Eric did not have a relationship with his biological father, and he felt that from a legal standpoint making us a single family would be easy. Even after the lack of support from the Mundy clan, I still saw no reason to cut Eric's paternal family off! They were a part of Eric's family history. Letting them stay involved made me question a great many things as Eric reached his young teens. Simple things would transpire to affect how Eric saw me and how he came to see his adopted father because of the Mundys' murmuring behind my back. My own close family members were guilty of sabotaging Eric's ability to bond with Jesse as well.

LESSONS LEARNED

- Look closely. Even as you go through your 'go through', there are people who want to support and help you.
- Heed good counsel only from those who are impartial. Don't share everything with everyone.
- Believe God's promise is that we all prosper in all areas of our lives.

CHAPTER 10

The Whispers Begin

When we moved to Detroit, Eric's aunt reached out to me because she wanted to meet my husband and catch up with her nephew. That one kind deed of allowing them to have full access to my child would have a profound impact on Eric and the way he viewed his adopted father as well as me in the years to come. Eric always visited his grandmother on his dad's side. He visited his aunts and uncle as well, even throughout the adoption process.

During visits, his paternal family members murmured, "Jesse is not your real dad." As Eric grew up, he noticed that Gerald visited his grandma's house, but he had no idea who he was.

I found out many years later after reading a newspaper article that when Eric asked who the stranger was, they simply said that he was "a friend of the family." They had no problem telling him that Jesse was not his "real" father, but they still rallied around Gerald and protected him. During all those years, before the truth finally came out, even as Gerald came over to "see" Eric during Eric's visits to Chicago, his family never told Eric that Gerald was his biological father. They made certain that Eric knew that he did not belong to Jesse, the man who had raised him as his own.

Not only had Gerald's family been telling Eric that Jesse wasn't his real dad, but some of my family members had been talking to Eric about it as well. One of my sisters was the main culprit. A few of my other sisters felt like they needed to tip off Eric and inform him of the secret, but a nosy neighbor took it to a new level. She worked at Eric's school, and I believe that when I presented the adoption papers when we enrolled him in his new school, she read those private documents and shared them with all of our neighbors. Eric was even hearing rumors and whispers from his classmates. For years he never mentioned these things to us. These rumors resulted in things taking a turn for the worse.

LESSONS
LEARNED

- As we began our new life, that was the time to explain to our son the changes that would be forthcoming.
- In the end, intentions, no matter how noble does not trump honest dialog.
- Failure to share such information information may lead your child getting it from someone else.

CHAPTER 11

Trouble in Paradise

During the early 1970s, Detroit was booming! There was more black homeownership in the D than in any other city in the United States. Working for the Big Three guaranteed steady work and loads of overtime. From the 1970s to the mid-1980s there were actually four thriving automakers. The Big Three were General Motors, Ford Motor Company, and Chrysler. American Motors held the fourth spot, but it was eventually bought by Renault, which was then absorbed by Chrysler. The year 1976 started off great for the Thomases. Soon after I learned to drive, I was hired at Ford Motor Company on July 6, 1976. We were riding high. After just two years of marriage, we had a home to call our own. It was in a great neighborhood that was surrounded by good schools. I was finally able to drive myself and Eric to my mom's place before I went to work. I finally was able to get off the bus system.

As a whole, our marriage was wonderful. We didn't experience most of the issues I had seen my mom undergo. However, matrimony was not without its ups and downs. We were both young when we married. Neither of us had been in a long-term relationship. Jesse had finished college and returned home, so he hadn't experienced long-term independence after college. We had lots of adjustments to make. We were both selfish in our own ways because we weren't used to sharing everything, and we did not understand how to compromise.

I didn't have any truly real trust in my husband. After my relationship with Eric's real father, I still struggled with truly believing men could be faithful. Leaving my friends and my comfort zone and moving to a city where Jesse was well known didn't help my insecurities. The old infidelity issues my mother experienced in her relationships clouded my mind whenever Jesse seemed overly friendly with other women. I had learned from watching through my eyes as a child that most disagreements ended with loud and mean-spirited words. Often physical confrontation followed. I was horrified that I would react and respond in the same ways that my mother had reacted.

I realized that being exposed to that type of behavior had brought some of that negative mindset to my marriage. Whenever I got frustrated, I would become argumentative, and my husband would clam up. I saw that our different ways of demonstrating how we felt during a disagreement or argument was having a negative impact on our relationship. I suggested marriage counseling; Jesse wasn't interested. After repeated pleadings, I finally decided that I needed to see a therapist, even if it meant going by myself. I found a nice lady therapist in Birmingham, Michigan. I was about twenty-five by then. Something had to give.

Jesse talked about how he wanted to begin to expand our family. We were both gainfully employed. Eric was happy and in a healthy space. However, at that point I had reservations about having another baby. If we couldn't get a lid on our disagreements, there was no way that I was having another child. It was time to seek some objective advice. I can remember going in to see my therapist for the first time. I was complaining about my husband not attending with me. I told her that I felt as if he really didn't care enough if he wasn't willing to attend the sessions with me. My therapist had a real conversation with me and told me that if I was truly interested in changing the way I interacted with my husband when there was conflict, he didn't need to be there with me.

Through our many sessions, I learned how to communicate effectively without my usual big blowup. My communicating differently would force Jesse to react differently. My therapist assured me of this. Therapy helped us grow as a couple. She and I talked a lot about my own upbringing because that's where we get a lot of our habits and views about life. We talked about how being from such a large family affected the way I looked at life. Working through my issues with her taught me what empathy really meant. I was able to take those things that I learned back to my marriage. My husband had been conditioned to respond to the things that I said during arguments. However, I had changed how I communicated with him which required another adjustment to our marriage; he had to adjust to the new version of me. He did not like it at first because he knew what to expect from the old me. Nevertheless, he soon realized that I had changed for the better, and he changed as well. After several months of weekly or biweekly sessions, my therapist told me that she felt that I was ready. She didn't need to see me anymore. She gave me some tips for effective communication. Most importantly, she told me that I needed to stop bottling up things about my husband that bothered me and that I needed to have a candid, frank conversation with him before it turned into a heated argument.

Understanding clearly how to talk with someone about problems that weighed heavily on my heart would be a tool that I didn't think I would need in any other relationships. Unfortunately, I would need it again for a relationship that I never thought would go sour.

LESSONS LEARNED

- Don't sweep serious issues under the rug. You must address them in order to resolve them and repair the relationship.
- Seek help from trusted friends, clergy or a health care provider.
- You will either be a part of the problem OR a part of the solution.
- You may need to be the 'change agent' in order to reach a positive resolution.

CHAPTER 12

The Bond of Friendship: Braile Street

As I began writing my chapter about Eric's early years in Detroit, I approached him and inquired who could best recall his early days on the block. At this point I realized that Eric had harbored a lot of secrets and that perhaps I really didn't know about all of the things that were going on in his head. I had to figure out which of his boyhood friends could give me a more honest viewpoint. Eric suggested that I speak to his best friend, Alonzo, so I reached out to him and explained my reason for the meet-up. We sat down and talked for several hours. I had no idea about many of the things that had transpired before Eric's period of re- bellion. I'm going to use Alonzo's words to give you some insight into what Eric was experiencing between the age of six which is when the two young boys first met all the way up to the changes that occurred after "Lonz," as Eric called him, moved away at the age of fourteen.

Ironically, both of these young men suffered for a time after their friendship ended. Alonzo and Eric shored one another up long before Bob King became E's new wingman. Bob would later introduce Eric to The Seventh-Day Adventist Church. He also introduced Eric to his (Eric's) future wife, Dilsey Mosley. Anyhow, Alonzo and my son had forged a strong bond. They held each other up, and they truly looked out for one another. Eric probably spent more time at his special friend's house than he did at ours; I now realize that it was his refuge, a place where he could get out of his head and just be accepted with no strings attached.

The Mundy Mitt
Eric and Alonzo played for PAL, the Police Athletic Association baseball league. Eric played first base and lead off in the line-up. One day Alonzo picked up his mitt, and he noticed that Eric had a different last name from the one he used at school; Eric Mundy was inked inside of his baseball mitt. Our neighbor, Tim Smith, a Detroit police officer, introduced Eric and some of the other kids on the block to the league out of the Northwest Activity in Detroit. He asked Eric whose mitt he was wearing and Eric told him, "It's mine. Eric Douglas Mundy was my before name." After Eric opened up and shared some personal information about himself, Lonzo said it allowed him to be able to open up more to Eric as well. His dad had experienced a serious slip and fall at work, and as a young husband and father, he was suffering emotionally because he wasn't able to maintain the family's previous lifestyle because of his inability to work.

With the two of them experiencing challenges in the home, a fast and solid friendship was born. There was a lot of jealousy and rivalry because Eric had so many things. We exposed him to things outside the neighborhood, so the youth, as well as their parents, worked to undermine our little family. When Alonzo spoke about how early Eric found out about his biological father, I was stunned to hear about the name inked on his mitt: Eric Douglas Mundy. He had never used the surname Mundy. Upon reflecting, I realized that the mitt had been a gift from the paternal side of his family. It was probably purchased during one of his visits to Chicago. So much deception. They must have felt certain that Eric would keep quiet. Couldn't they see the endgame—that when the secrets got too hard for my son to bear, there would be unimaginable suffering that would affect our entire family?

Of course, I never would have thought to go through all his belongings to see what he might have been given! I trusted them and didn't want to cut them out of his life. I would certainly take the prize for being the worst keeper of an "open secret". I never felt that the relationships required a closer look. Listening to Alonzo, I realized what a positive influence he was on Eric during the nine years that they lived on the same block.

Eric was blessed with a few very good friends. With all the turmoil in our home, I didn't recall that Alonzo's family had moved. Neither distance nor time strained the bonds of these two boys' friendship. Each of them went through some rough times. Alonzo began working at a motel where a coworker put illegal drugs in his food which caused him to react violently. He was then beaten by a policeman who did not understand what was happening to him. Eric was suffering under a delusion or false premise as well. He believed that we were awful parents because we had withheld his adoption information from him. In hindsight, he was right! Both of these young men suffered mightily. They both moved away from Michigan around the same age and went their separate ways, but they never lost the principles they had developed as boys.

Years later, Eric said that the Lord had spoken to him in a dream and showed him that Alonzo was experiencing a serious problem. Somehow, Eric was able to locate Niecey, Alonzo's sister, and he shared his vision with her. She told Eric that Alonzo was still suffering from the effects of the drugs he had been given. Eric said to her, "I need to see my friend." Fate interceded, and Alonzo was flying back to Detroit. Eric and Dee-dee were already at the

Detroit airport as they were preparing to return to Huntsville, Alabama. Somehow the two flights were located in the same terminal, and there was a little time between Alonzo's arrival and Eric's departure.

During the years we remained on Braile Street, Eric and his friends enjoyed tons of activities together; he played baseball on the same team with Lonzo, but for most of his afterschool and summer programs he attended alone. Eric never asked his friends to tag along to the movies with us either. There were programs and events he wanted to enjoy by himself. Years later Eric would make references in a TGIM about a movie I took him to see. It was called Chariots of Fire. I could not believe that he remembered it. That movie was about perseverance, honor, and friendships from an unusual place. We saw that movie in 1981. I grab hold of these special moments where Eric talks about the positive family memories throughout his childhood and teenage years because he certainly didn't show a lot of gratitude towards us during those times. Everybody knew that Eric was blessed but him. We would find out years later that some of his friends were wishing they could have the life that he lived. One of his friends Sam shared with us how he would have liked to have Jesse as his father when he was growing up. He always thought that my husband was a great dad to Eric.

Mother to Mother: The Bond of Friendship

I can't believe the carnage we created from trying to be great parents to our son. So much pain and misery! We tried everything in our power to help Eric get through his ordeal, so he could forgive us. We tried counseling and long talks with him on why we didn't share the information about his adoption. Jesse even spoke to our son and said," E, you are my son, and that will never change." I sought counseling and took Tough Love classes to try and set ground rules and yet he held firm in the way that he felt about us. We had the resources, so we decided to move.

What I did not understand was that you can't run away from all the ugliness that transpires in your life by changing your physical location. Even with our love for our child, we had screwed up big-time! We felt moving would allow us to have a do-over. We thought that maybe Eric would rethink his views if we all had a chance to walk away from the dirty truth he found out about while living on Braile Street.

We were so wrong. Nothing trumps the truth. Even when you come clean, you're fighting against all of the old assumptions, hurt and pain that person is carrying. Eric spoke his truth in his book *Secrets to Success*. We all experienced the unraveling of our lives as we knew it.

My readers may find what they perceive as glaring differences, but that's not so. My lens was colored with love and the need to protect Eric. With all the information he was given over a long period of time, his lens was clouded by our lies in not telling him the truth and nothing but the truth. Neither of us was forthright by withholding what we knew or suspected.

If you build your world on shaky ground, a stiff wind will cause it to collapse.

Our family life in Detroit was wonderful and filled with love. Jesse had a healthy relationship with Eric when Eric was a young boy, but as Eric heard more and more of how he came to be, the relationship turned ugly. Looking back, I can understand how and why he felt the way that he did. When he finally had the courage to ask if Jesse was his real dad, I thought I would tell him the truth. Eric felt my words justified everything he had been hearing from his extended family for a mighty long time.

The problem is that we don't live in a vacuum, so it was bound to come out! I remember watching an old mafia movie. A mafia boss ordered a hit out on one of his lieutenants. After the hit was carried out, the contract killer was called into a meeting. They then killed him. Before he was murdered, he asked the boss why he was about to be killed. The Mafia Don said, "Whenever two people know a secret, one has to die." So please know and understand that if anyone knows your secrets, you should be the one who comes clean because just as sure as night follows day, your secret will come to the light. I promise you that the pain and agony that comes from your secret being revealed by someone else can destroy your family! It was a long painful road to forgiveness. When you're in hurting, the only lens you see-through is pain, anger and disappointment. Please don't make the mistake I made. Someone is there playing the role of the 'truth speaker', and he or she will share the details with his or her own bias without considering how it will impact you or your child.

LESSONS LEARNED

- Having a true friend when you are going through your go-through is priceless.
- Being able to unload your thoughts to someone you trust allows you to vent.
- It's important to have structured activities to release pent up energy and aggression.
- No matter what, you must be the parent through it all. You can't undo what happened, but you can't vacate your role as a parent either.
- Even as they remain angry and defiant, they still want your love. Your love is the glue that will allow you to heal and mend the relationship.

CHAPTER 13

Eric the Leader

My firstborn was a high-energy, curious, go-go-go kind of kid. Early on, we found afterschool and weekend programs for him. I knew it was paramount in order for him to be well rounded. Back in the 1970s and 1980s, Detroit had a vast assortment of activities to keep children engaged. For several summers, Eric was a part of the National Youth Sports Program (NYSP). This was a federally funded platform held at two local colleges, Wayne State and the University of Detroit. NYSP consisted of educational classroom work during the first half of the day and all sports after lunch. Eric simply endured the first half, so he could attend the various sports clinics. He swam and ran track. He also played golf, football, and baseball.

Eric also attended a summer program called DAPCA which was geared towards teaching children about science and engineering. We made sure that Eric was not hanging out on the block all day while we worked. There were day-camps to keep him occupied as well. We also introduced him to the summer go-away camp Joy of Jesus. Eric went there for the first time at the age of nine. I can recall one moment very clearly when I dropped him off at a campus so that he could get on the bus for camp. He got on the bus, but as the bus was pulling off the parking lot, Eric was running to the back of the bus. He pressed his body against the rear window, and his face was full of tears. I had lied about his age in order to get him into the camp program. Eric was a real shorty, so I felt terrible about lying to get him in. I thought that he was way too young to go away from home for a week. I felt that I had made a colossal mistake. I started to cry as well. I turned to my husband and said, "Let's just stop the bus and get him off. You can see he's crying. It's obvious that he doesn't want to go."

Jesse said, "No, we're not stopping that bus. Eric's going. You've done your research, and we know that everything is going to be alright." Jesse reminded me that Trevor, one of his Thomas cousins, had gone to this camp several times, and he had some great experiences.

He said, "Because it's our son's first go-away camp, you are nervous." I had no real concerns about anything out of the ordinary happening to him while he was away. I was early to the pickup spot on the day the campers were due back. As the bus rolled to its stop, I was right at the bottom of the steps! Of course, I was a nervous wreck; I wondered how things had gone for him. It bothered me the whole week that I didn't stop the bus to get him off because I knew that he didn't want to go. I watched in horror as my child rushed down the steps towards me. After being gone seven whole days, he was still crying. Oh my God, I thought. I couldn't believe it; my son was still crying! I felt tears well up in my eyes as I pulled him close. I felt like a heel. I should've followed my first instinct and made my husband stop the bus and get my kid off of it. I could only imagine how he had suffered being away for all that time. He looked pitiful. I asked, "Son, what happened to you while you were away? Did someone bother you at camp? Please talk to me!"

Eric answered through his tears, "Mom, I didn't want to come home. I was having fun. Mom, we learned how to fish. We got up early in the morning every day, so we could earn our Polar Bear badge by swimming in the cold lake at sunrise! Sometimes we slept in tents. Mom, Mom, it was so much fun. Can I go again?"

Go back? I was too stunned to speak! I was relieved to know that he didn't have any bad experiences, and I was so happy to see that he had such a wonderful time. After allowing us to reconnect, one of the camp counselors, David, came up to me and said that they wanted to have Eric come back next week. Now, mind you, this camp was funded by some church agency, so we paid very little. Because of the high demand, they didn't allow a child to go more than once per season. My antenna went up immediately. I asked David, "So why do you want my son to come back?"

He chuckled, "There's nothing improper going on. I can assure you." I still wasn't convinced. I had read somewhere about trouble with some boys going to these 'sleepaway' camps. Since it was on my heart when I saw him crying, my first thoughts were that something bad had happened to my baby. So I asked David point-blank, "Why do you want Eric to return to camp for another session?"

Fortunately, David was an understanding young man and he said, "I'll tell you why."

David told me that within a couple of days of Eric's first visit, they learned that Eric had a great deal of influence on the other campers. Even the older boys gravitated to him and followed his lead. "Once we realized Eric was a positive catalyst to our camp, and we saw how he was able to herd the different groups together—the black and white city kids with those from the rural areas—we saw him as a positive role model. That's why we would love to have him come back," he added.

We witnessed that same leadership ability in our son as well. Eric had the heart of a lion. Our doorbell always rang early on the weekends, no matter the weather, with some young man or another looking to see if Eric could come out for a pickup football or baseball game. The boys always wanted Eric to be a part of their team. They pulled him away from our block so much that we eventually put a basketball hoop on the garage. I was always more comfortable with him closer to home. I'd rather have our place as the gathering spot than to have him running around with some of the boys who did not have a lot of parental guidance. I told David that if Eric wanted to go back, he was more than welcome.

LESSONS LEARNED

- Expect pain and anger to be heaped on you by those you have hurt.
- Even during turmoil, you must maintain structure.
- Don't give up on mending the relationship. It will take time.
- A display of righteous indignation will only make matters worse.

PART III

THE SECRET
COMES OUT

"Sometimes that EX is ourselves, and we need to cut ties with
who we were. Time to come clean!"
— *Unknown*

CHAPTER 14

The Phone Call

I remember being at work and going through my normal work routine when my phone rang. Eric said, "Mom, I have something to ask you."

Then he said 6 words, "Mom, is Dad my real dad?" It would change our family forever.

I could feel his pain through the phone. I was silent for I don't know how long. Eric then said, "Mom, whatever you say, I will believe you." Eric was twelve years old at the time; he was almost thirteen. It was painful to hear him ask that question, but I would not continue to withhold the truth from him about being adopted. Nonetheless, I could not tell my son the entire story about how dysfunctional his biological father was. Mentioning any negativity surrounding his "real" father would not alter the truths that I had to confess. I told Eric my truth that day. I told Eric that his birth certificate had been altered to allow Jesse to adopt him and to give him his new name.

In the previous chapters I mentioned how the whispers began surrounding Eric's adoption. He suspected something long before he asked me and the more he suspected that those murmurings held some truth to them, his rebellious behaviors started to ramp up. After my secret came out, it was safe to say that 'all hell broke loose'.

We struggled mightily after that day Eric called me. We tried extremely hard to repair our son's trust in us and to show him that while we were guilty of lying or omitting the truth, we had no evil intent. Our son continued his battles with us. He became more negative and rebellious. Eric knew what to do to make me upset, and that's exactly what he did moving forward. He was very defiant, and he did not listen. Despite his behavior and attitude, we did not throw in the towel or give up on getting him the help he needed.

We decided to seek counseling for Eric. We were trying to do everything we could to help him. When I sought counseling from a therapist in Detroit, Eric had issues with her. We tried an older female counselor, but Eric just sat there and would not discuss what was on his mind. Someone in the same practice as this counselor suggested that Eric sees a male therapist because the female therapists weren't able to reach him. Our third therapist was a male high school counselor, but that didn't work out either.

Our home life continued to crumble, but my husband stayed true to his belief in his role in Eric's life. He continued to try and offer guidance to Eric to help him through the rites of manhood. He taught him how to cut grass the proper way and how to change the oil in the car, among other things. Jesse is a big guy but not a big talker. For the most part, when he had to discipline our son, Jesse remained the calm person he was. I, on the other hand, was often in a rage. I just couldn't understand Eric's extreme level of ingratitude. I often yelled at him, listing all of the sacrifices that Jesse and I had both made to provide a better life for him. Sadly, I actually understood little of Eric's state of mind.

All he needed was the truth. He should have received it early on, and we should have been the stewards of that truth. But how do you tell a child that his father doesn't really want to be in his life? When Gerald walked away, he never looked back. He went on to have three or four more children, and they were all by different women. My ego didn't want my child to know that I could be attracted to such an irresponsible soul. I believed that if Eric knew the truth in that I had chosen such a character, it would somehow diminish me in his eyes. In reflecting, I often wondered if that was the main reason I never told the whole truth.

The Chaos Continues

Eric remained angry with us and not just for withholding information regarding his "real" father. Our son was hellbent on behaving like an adult, although we were supporting and taking care of him like he was a child. He bristled at house rules. We believed in rules and regulations. Jesse and I imposed a curfew, expected obedience, and had expectations regarding education. Most of the young people in our area lived with both parents, but their kids had more freedom and less structure. That difference subjected Eric to vicious teasing by other kids because Jesse was not his "real" father. Other kids, who were not disciplined by their parents, started talking in Eric's ear about how Jesse had no authority over him. Eric believed them. And somehow I was a villain for working with Jesse in helping to keep our family structure.

Eric's bad attitude followed him to the classroom as well. After we had enrolled him in the traditional neighborhood public school, we noticed that he wasn't faring too well. We then explored other educational systems. We even looked at the idea of homeschool. When Eric struggled with reading, we purchased the book *Let's Read* and incorporated the linguistic style to teach our son to read. I was quite familiar with that method, as I was a product of the late 1950s public school system, where I learned to read using sight words. At some point, I realized that Eric just did not like to read; he was just skimming through the books. Well, my answer to his shenanigans was for me to read the book as well. I would ask certain questions, and I would know if he had just read the first couple of pages and then maybe two pages or chapters in the middle and the ending. Whatever it took, that's what I was going to do.

We enrolled him into a parochial school. That was a dreadful fit. Eric had too much energy and lasted there just one year! At one of his many Saturday programs, I was complaining about how we were asked not to bring Eric back to Saint Bede's Catholic School. Someone asked if we had heard about Detroit's School Choice System, the Open School in particular. Open enrollment was approaching, and one of the mothers gave me the necessary information. The schools made it difficult to gain admittance in order to discourage black families.

By chance, I went over to the school a few days before the enrollment date. I wasn't familiar with the area, so I wanted to be sure I knew how to get there. To my surprise, a line had already formed. People had actually pitched tents so they could stand there and 'hold' their children's spot for admission. Families were working in shifts with their friends to secure spots. Of course, I flew home to convince my husband, "Hey, we have got to get in line now!" I hooked up with a couple of families at the end of the line who had not formed any alliances. I asked if we could take turns so that we could secure all of our children's spots. Everyone that I asked agreed, and we were assigned the times we had to report for roll call! To make matters more difficult, some of the people who were first in line decided that they would go across every so often and demand to see our numbers. We were diligent, and by the grace of God, Eric and our group got selected. We found out later that even if your number was first, children who had other siblings who could fill a class opening were chosen over a single child. We loved that school because its approach was similar to that of Montessori schools. Their methods were very engaging, and they motivated students to gain interest in learning again.

Once again this was our attempt to get Eric whatever help he needed in order to get him back on track. This school didn't work out for him either.

LESSONS LEARNED

- The past has reared its ugly head.
- You have to deal with the consequences and repercussions from the past.
- It was time to go all in. Nothing can be off the table to repair the relationship.
- You think you're doing something to shield your children, but your children think that you're withholding something from them.

CHAPTER 15

The Move to Southfield

In 1986, Jesse asked again, "Why don't we move to Southfield?" This wasn't the first time he brought it up, but I wasn't ready the first time. It crossed my mind several times that maybe Eric's hard core behaviors were magnified by his circle of friends in the area. This time when Jesse asked I took it into consideration. We had exhausted all the options that we felt would help our son through his emotional meltdown. Perhaps a new environment would help him. We met with our financial advisor to be sure we could afford the area to which we wished to move. He worked with Merrill Lynch, and as fate would have it, he sat on Southfield's zoning board meetings. Our guy informed us that Walter P. Reuther Freeway was being extended eastward and that it would divide Southfield into two different segments. He suggested that we move north of Eleven Mile Road as many of the homes south of Eleven Mile Road would be razed to build it.

We found a beautiful four-bedroom home in the Twickenham subdivision. This home was a better fit for us because by then we had three children. We happily moved in. We were thinking that the problems would go away somehow because Eric's circle of influence had changed. We enrolled him in Southfield Lathrup High School. However, it wasn't long before he found like-minded friends at school. Two of his friends were disrespectful in a cavalier way. It seemed that because Eric bashed us, they in turn were disrespectful to us and our home.

I came home once to find one of the boys sitting on my finished wood console in the hallway. He was wearing studded jeans, and he had no regard for scratching my furniture. It was obvious that Eric had already shared his disdain for us; otherwise, they would not have behaved so disrespectfully! I tore into him and said, "Young man, when you're in my home, you will not disrespect it. Go sit in a chair or stand up." They left abruptly. I told Eric that he was wrong to allow his friends to show disregard for our home. Later, we took our youngest two to Chicago for a visit. Eric didn't want to go with us. My gut told me to cut our trip short.

We came home a day early, and we knew immediately that something was wrong. The house was spotless. Eric never picked up anything until you forced him. My radar went off, and we started going through the rooms and personal stuff to figure out what had occurred. Clearly, something improper had happened. We started with our bar; everything seemed to be in place. Eric rarely cooked, but I peeped into the refrigerator. We then took a quick look in the freezer. It was almost empty. Jesse asked what had happened to the six New York steaks we had purchased at the butcher shop. Before we had decided to visit Chicago, we had planned a family Barbeque and the steaks were going to be dinner. Next, we went to the garage to look in the garbage cans. They were stuffed with paper plates and empty beer and wine bottles! It was clear he had thrown a party in our absence! When I tried to talk to him, of course, he was disrespectful to me. Jesse got involved and said, "Man, don't disrespect your mother." They began arguing.

Dad said, "You know the rules!"

Eric said, "I don't have to listen to you; you are not my father!"

Jesse replied, "You'll obey my rules, and if you can't, then you'll have to leave."

Eric shouted, "I hate you!" I can't truly recall all of what happened next, but he pushed his father during the chaos. Jesse grabbed him. They tussled for a moment, and the subject of manhood came into their heated argument.

"There's only one man in this house," said Jesse. They tussled a bit more until Jesse put Eric in a headlock. Eventually, Eric pulled loose, and as he was running to exit the house through the garage, he turned back and yelled, "I'm never coming back, and I hate both of you."

There were numerous disagreements leading up to this point. The entire home was saturated with stress and tension. At that point I knew that I had done everything within a mother's power to diffuse the arguments and yet honor our rules and value system. Eric's way of dealing with his knowledge that he was adopted had created the perfect storm. His circle of influence didn't care about school. They had strained relationships with their parent or parents. At this point, those friends were hell-bent on doing what they wanted. They were doing their thing without the understanding that independence came with a price.

In an attempt to be good parents, we gave Eric an older car of ours. It was our old Ford Escort. He was still so angry that he allowed his friends to drive the car after we explained the legal and monetary consequences of allowing anyone outside the family to drive it. The car jumped the curb and busted the axle. After we had it repaired, I sold it. He lost a lot of his freedom by being defiant. I did understand his willingness to let people use the car because so many people were looking out for him. He didn't want to listen to us explain how it would've cost us dearly if someone had been injured or killed. So much happened as we moved to try and patch up our broken family.

Eric, You Have to Leave

The night that I asked my son to leave home had been a long time coming. It had begun long before we moved from Braille Street. My husband really didn't have anything to do with Eric being put out. Although they did have the confrontation, the road to Eric's departure started because Eric was out of control and totally disrespectful. His father didn't ask Eric to leave; I did because Eric was bound and determined to focus simply on his pain and his pain only. I'm still not sure what happened to precipitate the final blow up. My recollection was the continued lack of respect and regard coupled with the stress of caring for my mother-in-law. She moved in with us because she was grievously ill. She had pancreatic cancer. I was an emotional wreck, and there would be no compromise between Eric and me. Our girls were walking around stressed and on edge, knowing that more rounds of arguments were coming. Jesse's way of dealing with his mother's fatal diagnosis was to shut down. His calm demeanor was absent at the time that we all needed it the most.

I managed to get Eric to come back to help out with his sisters while I tried to get Grandma Shirley situated. He did, and one evening he decided to start a fire in the fireplace. He didn't realize that dampers were closed, so the house quickly filled with smoke. His grandma panicked, and after I calmed her down, I admonished him. His response, an angry outburst, was the proverbial straw that broke the camel's back.

Everything fell on my head. I was unable to absorb any more pain. In my heart, I knew that I had been a good mother, and I knew that Jesse had been a good father. Jesse's ability to always remain objective helped stabilize any disagreements. I, on the other hand, was like Eric in that we saw everything from a subjective, emotional viewpoint. My son and I just saw the situation from harshly opposing views. The level and tone of our argument had reached the boiling point. I remember that my husband wasn't even present the day I asked Eric to leave that last time; he was on the afternoon shift. I simply went to my purse and pulled out all the bills I had. With tears in my eyes, I told my firstborn, "You have to go." I cried afterward. I called my husband to tell him what I had done. I asked Eric to go; it was simply time. We had used every resource to repair our relationship with our son.

After I cried, a sense of peace came over me. I said to myself, "I've thrown in the towel. There's nothing more that I can do." After my husband came home from work, he asked me, "Are you sure this is the right thing to do? Where will he go?"

I simply said, "I can no longer live with the distress of knowing that no matter what we said or did, it would not make a hill of beans' worth of difference." Eric was rigid, full of disdain and disrespect.

During her brother's acts of defiance, Neco, my oldest daughter, suffered so much. She was torn between her love for her brother and her respect for us. I told Jesse that if Eric was somehow allowed to stay, his negative disposition would poison her, and we would lose her as well. Eric was going to stand his ground, and it would be the death of me if we did not separate ourselves. I had a responsibility to protect my daughter's mental state as well. Neco was just eight years old. She did not deserve the fallout from this. I knew how mightily the adoption reveal affected him. Under normal circumstances, Eric would not have acted out in a way that would cause Neco pain or harm. In his present state of mind, he put everything aside except for anger and pain. I had to be the one to put a stop to this animosity because his sisters suffered collateral damage from it all.

My Breaking Point

During my company's Christmas gala, I looked over at Jesse, and he appeared to be drunk. He denied it, but he was slurring his words; he seemed to be listing to one side. As he walked, I noticed him staggering. I had never seen Jesse drunk, but looking at the signs, my brain said that he was. I was angry and embarrassed, so we left abruptly. We had a huge fight that night. Jesse was insisting that he had only had two drinks. Early the next day, as he was coming downstairs, he slipped and tumbled to the bottom of the stairs.

I remember thinking, "There is no way he could still be drunk!" I raced over to him and asked, "What is going on with you?"

He looked puzzled and cautiously made his way to the den. He murmured, "I don't know." We decided at some point to go to the emergency room because he kept falling. His sense of balance was out of whack. As he examined Jesse, the emergency room doctor wasn't very kind. I nervously asked, "Do you have any idea what's happening?" The doctor replied, without concern or facts, that Jesse may have had a stroke. He was answering my questions as if my husband was invisible. We followed up with Jesse's primary doctor who suggested we see a neurologist. This new ordeal, on top of everything else, worried me. Several months after Eric left, his father was diagnosed with multiple sclerosis.

All of the conflict and life-altering situations tore me into pieces. I couldn't understand why I was held accountable for fixing everybody's issues. I had taken on everyone's burdens, but no one could see how they were destroying me. Only by God's grace was I able to avoid a complete nervous breakdown during these trials. Those people that rallied around me regarding my war with my son argued that Eric was wrong and ungrateful, while Eric had his own camp telling him that we were wrong and that we were liars who didn't deserve his respect. When I spewed my poisonous words and woes, everybody rallied behind me. I felt convicted, even while I held anger toward those with whom Eric shared his pain. These people rallied against me.

Those were the hardest days any mother could ever experience outside of a mother having her child perish in her lifetime. I was at the lowest point in my life. Even with all that I had endured, the gulf between my son and me was worse than death. Death would have ended my suffering from our love/hate relationship. It had rendered me a shell of my former happy self. I wouldn't wish those feelings of indescribable pain and loss coupled with anger and a sense of hopelessness on anybody. It was a vicious cycle that would not end for the longest of time. Another one of my sisters died, and I feared that I would be next. I didn't want that to happen without having restored the love my firstborn and I once shared. We remained in our battle. We were somehow unable to bring it to positive closure. Yet, God was merciful in the end.

I didn't go to a support group. I tried to become superwoman/supermom. I had to keep working. What if Jesse was never able to return to his position at General Motors? I was pretending that I wasn't falling apart with all of this happening. I was being estranged from my first-born. I was carrying the guilt of leaving my two youngsters at home knowing their dad wasn't truly able to do much. I was trying to cope with my youngest daughter's reactions to all that was going on. She had a meltdown as well. She would cry, and no one could console her when she came home from school day after day. She wanted her mama, and I wasn't able to be there for her. My prolonged absence caused her to retreat emotionally.

I went to my boss and asked for a temporary schedule change. He allowed me to work a split shift, 10:00 a.m.to 6:00 p.m. For several years, I was blessed to see my youngest off to school, and then I would be back home by suppertime. I was able to help with homework and see and put my daughters to bed. My brain raced so much under this pressure that I developed insomnia, so

I took sleeping pills. When I found myself taking Ambien on the way home from work so it would be in my system, I knew I needed help. The Lord was with me that day! Traffic was smooth and flowing. There were no delays. God only knows what would have happened had I fallen asleep at the wheel. I still can't believe I was stupid enough to do that. But when you're sleep-deprived, your brain is not functioning logically. All I wanted was to be able to fall right to sleep the moment my head hit my pillow. I finally sought the help I needed. I found a sleep clinic at Henry Ford Hospital, and that's when I was told that I was suffering from depression and anxiety as well. I saw a counselor and learned some coping skills. From the outside, I looked perfectly normal, but inside I was an emotional wreck! No one, not even my immediate family knew the intensity of my pain and suffering. I had developed a stoic façade, but I was falling to pieces inside.

It took me many years to move past all the disappointment, bitterness, and anger. I had no one who I could really talk to. I became cold and angry. In my eyes, I had done everything humanly possible for my son as far as raising him well and with love, but I could not have foreseen the fallout from not telling him about his real father. It never occurred to us that Eric would eventually find out the truth. During his visits to Chicago, he never once mentioned that he had ever seen or heard about his father from his paternal family. I thought that protecting him from the bitter truth was best. Lying created a perfect storm. All of those people got into his head with their version of the truth. He was too young to be dealing with that. I painfully learned that the truth should have been spoken. I should have been the one to tell Eric because my sharing it would have come without spite, malice, or misguided intentions.

Mother to Mother: Speak the Truth
Going over my words, I understood that because of my own blended family, we had learned to navigate through these different relationships forged by our various stepfathers. I never had a problem with extended relationships. My reconnection with my

father was a Godsend. I was happy to know his side of the family. Visiting with my father's extended family helped me understand a lot of things about myself and why I acted or behaved in certain ways.

What I don't understand is why, although I allowed Eric to know his father's family, I didn't share the truth with Eric about his father. I should have paid more attention to his mood when he returned from his visits. I should have asked questions.

I told myself that I didn't really share more with Eric about his biological father because it had been brought to my attention that Gerald was on hard drugs. In hindsight, I could see that he was probably using them when we first met. I was naïve, and I had trouble believing that I could not see it while we were dating. Maybe some part of my heart or brain didn't want Eric to know the bitter truth– that his biological father was a drug addict.

I had kept the truth hidden from my son. My reaction was completely emotional. Much too late, I realized that by lying through omission, I had diminished my ability to be seen as honorable and forthcoming to my son. I don't know how I could have thought that by allowing Eric to see his paternal relatives, nobody was going to say anything to him about his real father. I was so wrong! They had been talking to him about his father for a very long time. The thing that was so damaging and that hurt me the most was that Eric's paternal family didn't tell him the whole truth; they just told him half-truths and innuendos. Eric kept all this chatter to himself.

I wondered how long he listened to their words before he started to hate his adoptive father and me for the truth that we had withheld. Their words didn't build Gerald up in Eric's eyes. When Eric finally realized that Gerald was always there when he visited, posing as a "friend" of the family, for a time, Eric lost respect for him, too.

All those things we all did or did not do led to our having to put our son out of our home at the age of sixteen. No one could have foreseen how it altered his relationship with his sisters. The wrath Jesse and I received from my own family for kicking Eric out was challenging to endure.

Now, I can't blame it all on his paternal side of the family. If the truth be known, a couple of my sisters and other close relatives approached him as well with their version of the truth. Some of their innuendos were more wicked. Eric was repeatedly asked if he remembered a time when Jesse wasn't his dad. They kept asking him if he remembered a time when he had a different last name. Eric could remember, and he had snatches of memories that would blow your mind. I'm sure he can recall a time when Jesse was not in our lives because he wasn't there every night like I was. Family members may claim, for whatever reason, that they told him because it was the right thing to do. It was not the right thing to do nor will it ever be. When you truly love someone, you never cause them this kind of pain. If you think an injustice is being done, you don't go to the child. You take it to the person whom you feel is responsible for that injustice. Neither my sisters nor my son's relatives on his father side ever approached me to ask me what I was going to do regarding sharing the truth of my son's adoption. No, they were all dishonorable. They went behind my back and damn near destroyed my son.

The backlash started in earnest during his middle school years. Eric speaks of those years of anger when he felt he was unwanted and a mistake and that I just couldn't end my pregnancy. Nothing could have been further from the truth. I loved my son from the moment he was born—even before he was born. I was ashamed that I had gotten pregnant because I thought I was too smart for that. But the unthinkable did happen! However, it never changed the fact that I cherished him and was often tested in my desire to protect him.

My keeping his biological father's identity a secret gave him the impression that he was a mistake. Yet, all those people who felt that it was their obligation to share the truth with him—without telling him the whole truth—only muddied the waters. I'm guilty of having given them the ammunition.

Years later, I was asked if I was ever going to tell Eric the truth. I still cannot answer truthfully whether or not I would've shared the adoption news with Eric or his sisters. Who knows? It's out now. What I do believe is that God's plan was carried out as ordered. I have witnessed too many instances of people—men in particular—being healed by hearing Eric's own experiences of being born out of wedlock and the associated shame and anger he felt. As painful as our lives were for such a long time, it was not for naught. That burning pain he suffered because we had withheld the truth about his birth father has purified and repaired so many broken souls. God is good all the time—yes, even throughout our trials.

LESSONS LEARNED

- You are the one that can help your child become whole, but there will come a time when you've done all that you can.
- A parent's love can strengthen her offspring or make them weak. We must learn from the animal kingdom. They pour everything into their babies knowing that there will come a time where their babies will have to leave the nest.
- We must do the same. There is a time to say, "It's time to go."
- When we enable our children instead of preparing them, it's going to be hard to let go. This cripples them.

PART IV

LIFE AFTER
THE SECRET

"When everything feels like an UPHILL struggle, just think of the view from the top."
— *Unknown*

CHAPTER 16

Eric Goes to Oakwood

Eric left to go to Oakwood College in 1989. I remember him telling us of his decision to leave approximately a week before he actually left. I was aware that he was in the GED program, and I actually informed him of his results when he passed. However, I didn't know he had plans to leave. Even after he left for college, it would take time for him to rid himself of his anger and sense of betrayal. During one visit home from Oakwood, Eric brought some new friends with him. There was that old familiar heavy tension in the air. One young man seemed confused that I was nice and polite. I imagined that Eric had painted a very unflattering picture of this family, and yet again my son brought friends to our home without any notice. I decided not to be defensive toward his friends this time. Instead, I said, "Young man, you seemed to be perplexed. Who were you expecting to see—an old, worn-out woman in a house dress with gold teeth and a .38 pistol in her house dress pocket?" He laughed, and that diffused the heavy tension in the air.

Eric was missing us, and even in the thrall of his pain, he reached out the best way he could by visiting during a break. I had begun to look at our situation from a different perspective, and I was grateful for my small measure of growth. His approach to staying connected left a lot to be desired, but even though he was still angry, he reached out to connect with us. Eric and Dee-dee got married at the beginning of their second year of college. I thought they were too young to get married, but I didn't fight it.

While in Huntsville, Eric began an outreach program teaching a GED program called Break The Cycle. He started it in the neighborhood public housing complex. Jesse and I were very happy to see the impact he had in the community. He was also traveling and speaking to different churches at this time. We were happy, but I wouldn't say we were necessarily surprised. As I mentioned in previous chapters, we knew early on that Eric was a leader and that he had the ability to draw people to him. To see him operating in his gifts made us so proud!

Eric had his academic troubles at Oakwood, but he never let them keep him from reaching his goal. I'll never forget the day he finally graduated from Oakwood. They positioned me right by the podium where they shook the graduates' hands and handed out the diplomas. His friend LD jockeyed me through the crowd towards the front row where the graduates exited the stage. As Eric walked off the stage, LD told me to lean over the railing. Eric placed his award around my neck and said, "Mom this is for you." Jesse and I were over the moon and excited to be a part of this magical moment. He finally finished what he started years ago and earned his Bachelor of Arts degree. I will never forget that moment. This is when things started to get better for us. He even did something very powerful to display his love and appreciation for Jesse. It would be years later, but Eric presented Jesse with a plaque for the Best Dad award at a Men's Day in Detroit. It was a very heartwarming experience, even for those who were there to witness it. Eric started to get choked up when he talked about how this 'giant of a man' took him in as his own. These types of moments highlighted growth and forgiveness.

As time went on after Eric's graduation, Eric's family increased, but we still had lingering old hurts to shed. Because of the existing tension, we missed the birth of our first and only grandson. Although we were not present during our second grandchild's birth, my youngest daughter and I went to Huntsville to meet our little princess while she was still an infant. We did not make a good impression! On our second day, Mallori, my daughter, became ill. By day three, I was sick as well. And before you knew it, Dee-dee had contracted our bug. Then Eric and both of the grandchildren caught it! Not a good impression to make when you feel that you're not truly a welcomed guest.

Dee-dee's mom traveled the road from Detroit to Huntsville often, and I always felt bad that I was unable to visit more. Mrs. Mosley was blessed to be retired, and she had more freedom. I, on the other hand, still had a child in middle school and was still working at Ford. Nothing seemed to correct the situation until one day, out of the blue, we got a call from Eric. He told us that he had a chance to move back to Michigan. He was offered the position of Academic Advisor at Michigan State! This move is what I consider to be the catalyst to repairing our relationship.

LESSONS LEARNED

- We must choose to take a second look at a familiar relationship and make the shift in improving that relationship.
- I had to become the change agent in order to get to a healthier place.
- We must become sensitive to others by viewing situations through their lenses.

CHAPTER 17

Eric Sees Clearly Now

"I can see clearly now," Eric wrote in his book The Secret to Success. He was reflecting on being a parent. Our son finally understood that we had set boundaries and expectations for him because we wanted to protect him. We had tried to set a foundation so that once he left home, he had a blueprint that he could follow to be successful in whatever endeavor he chose.

During his teenage years, Eric could not understand our processes. Each time we set a curfew, assigned chores, or insisted on rules and regulations, he chafed. Knowing that the man who raised him wasn't his biological father just increased his resentment.

I often felt that Eric focused his wrath more on me. He felt that I had betrayed him because I went along with his father in insisting on creating boundaries for him. Eric saw family and friends who had financial stability. He saw them give lavish gifts to their children, yet they didn't teach those children values and guidance— not even those values that helped the parents themselves reach their goals. Our family was the odd duck in many ways, but we did not yield on raising our son to understand the need for principles, rules and guidelines, and, above all, integrity. I would not allow my son to grow up without moral guidelines. I was going to break the generational curses under which I had grown up. My son would not grow up to behave in such a disrespectful manner. Eric rebelled against our principles. He had several friends who were so spoiled that their moms would defer their own desires just to please the kid. Eric had the nerve to ask me why I asked Dad what he wanted for dinner sometimes. I replied, "What do you mean?" It seemed that his friend Jeff set the tone for family meals in his home. Another friend's father gave him a bucket filled with hundreds and hundreds of Susan B. Anthony coins. That kid had everything but parents who spent quality time with him. There were other boys who got caught up in selling or using drugs. Most were boys without supervision. Only later, after Eric had his own children, would he understand what the principles of parenting truly meant.

We would finally laugh about the summer of 1984 which was the year I turned 32 and was pregnant with my youngest daughter! Eric was a teenager then. Eric thought that I was old, and that I shouldn't be pregnant. Of course, I asked my son a question when he turned thirty-two. It was a question that we will never forget.

"May I ask you a personal question, son?"

"Of course, Mom," he replied.

"Are you and Dee-dee still having sex?" It took him a minute for it to register, but he burst out laughing! "Mom," he said, "every kid thinks their parents are old when they're teenagers! And they do not want evidence that their parents are having sex! It was so embarrassing." It must be a Thomas thing. If Jayda, Eric's daughter, sees her parents hug, kiss, or even cuddle, she groans and laughingly pulls them apart.

LESSONS LEARNED

- Your hard work as a parent is not in vain. They ARE listening.
- You will be rewarded as you see them become more independent.
- Press on by giving them the tools and wisdom that got you through your own life trials.

CHAPTER 18

Eric's Homecoming

So as stated before, Eric called to say he and his family were moving back to Lansing, Michigan. He had been offered a fellowship from Michigan State to earn his master's degree in Education Administration. At this point, he had been gone from home for more than a decade. To some degree, our relationship was still damaged. Eric always felt that I should have a conversation with Dee-dee to see what our differences were. I felt that any ill will she may have had against me originated from her love of him and how Eric chose to describe the incidents that caused him to leave home. I never met Dee-dee during their courtship. She was another one of his secrets. I felt that he had played a part in the way she perceived me just as he had done with his other friends. Based on their perception of me, I didn't expect anything different from her. I was not willing to broach that conversation with her. My selfish wish was to see and spend more time with my grandchildren.

Old issues between us still waxed and waned. Old hurts and dis-appointments just would not die that final death. While his dad and I were visiting out West, Eric called me. Jesse would say later that he knew something was really wrong because I left the room to continue our conversation. I don't even remember exactly what the conversation was about, but Eric was still saying, "Mom, you know that if you have issues, then you need to communicate." I just didn't feel that it was my place to address any issues that I had with Dee-dee regarding letting us have our grandchildren visit us. I did not want a short drive-by visit with them. I felt that Eric was the reason for a great deal of the animosity. I didn't see how my initiating a conversation would make any difference. During that heated conversation, I said to him, "This is the last time that you are going to make me cry." I was just so fed up that I was expected to be the only agent of change. Just in my own way, I never spoke to Dee-dee about my views. There would be no mediation from Eric. Psychologically, we were alike. My son was my little mini-me. Even so, we had not bridged that gap after all those years. "No more tears," I said. I didn't take those words literally. Oddly it wasn't so much that I would no longer allow Eric to make me cry over our past. I quit dwelling on things that would make me cry about our relationship. It had been such a long time, and I was just weary of it all. By then, I had lost three of my sisters to cancer. It troubled me to think that I could be next. All this time had passed, and yet neither of us uttered an apology. There was no open dialogue to get closure—just a wariness of what could come up during our visits or conversation. I wore a heavy cloak of bitterness draped over my shoulders. I decided that I would not lament over it any-more. I would just quit looking at what went wrong. I just decided to move forward.

My beloved grandchildren were very close! Lansing was only about eighty miles due west of Southfield. We had never gotten them to visit during their school breaks. Whenever they came from Huntsville to visit Dee-dee's mom, Grandma Glenda in De-troit, their parents never told us. But Grandma Glenda would call me and let me know that they were in town. I would be so angry that we weren't offered any real access to our grandchildren. I would say to my son, "I can't believe the kids can't come visit the Thomas side."

But my grandchildren were now within my reach, and they would be the catalyst for me truly putting things behind me once and for all.

I hatched a plan with Jesse, and then I asked Eric if we could meet up on I-96 in Howell, Michigan. Howell was the halfway point between Southfield and East Lansing. I found a park-and-ride spot off I-696 where people left their cars to ride in a carpool van. Eric and I put together a drop-off/ pickup schedule. Jesse and I looked forward to their visits, but it felt so much like a divorced couple's court order: scheduled visitation rights!

However, that was just the start! My grandchildren loved coming to visit, and we loved having them. We quickly established our little rituals. I always baked cupcakes and made Jalin's breakfast request of my famous oatmeal! Jesse introduced his first grandchild to fishing. Granddad also showed Jalin how to cut French fries the "Thomas" way (no skinny fries—thick steak fries was the way we Thomases did fries). The two of them experimented with different batter when they cooked chicken for our homemade chicken and waffles Sunday breakfast feast.

Soon, Eric, Dee-dee, and the kids began to drive down to visit. We began to have supper as a family for the holidays. Glenda Mosley had always come to our home for dinner, and we included her in our holiday meals before they headed over to visit her extended family. I started going all the way up to Lansing to get the kids and to babysit when Dee-dee went with Eric on his business trips or vacation.

I cherished every opportunity I had to spend with them because we had lost so much time when they were very young. Amazingly, although we didn't see them often during their formative years, they loved us back! I was able to pass on my love for reading to Jayda. I kept the same tradition I had started with my children. I looked for the top children's books. It was such a great feeling when we read the same book and discussed which characters touched us. Jalin, on the other hand, just wanted me to buy him video games. Like his father, he didn't care as much for reading. I did find him a few books that touched him, and I was proud of that. I was also proud that Grandpa Jesse was able to expose his grandson to something he loved doing as well. Fishing also allowed Jalin to bond with his uncle Cordel, Jesse's only brother.

My heart was full of joy. Our feud was finally over! My husband and I were still working, and our youngest daughter was still at home, but I no longer felt the unspoken censoring that we had been bad parents to our son.

During my own soul-searching, I came to the conclusion that my old mindset wasn't helping me get what I wanted, so I developed a different strategy. As our relationship improved, Eric and Dee-dee seem to be open to our suggestions on taking care of the grandchildren more often; I began to drive them all the way home. No more drop offs on the side of the highway! I spent time going to church with Eric and his family. Summers were the best. I don't drive at night, so in the summertime, I could stay as long as I was home by 9:00 p.m., whereas early darkness made staying later a little tricky in the winter and early spring. Somehow, we made it work because Eric and I realized that harmony is more important than being right.

In Algebra, two negatives equal a positive after cross cancellation or something. Mathematics is not my strong subject! Taking two negative situations rang true as it allowed the two of us to finally repair our relationship. Eric will say, of course, that it was me who delayed our coming together, but I don't agree. Eric and I worked towards putting our own issues aside because we understood bringing our families to a healthy happy place trumped everything. Jesse never took sides throughout the entire ordeal. It seems like he always knew it would work itself out somehow.

One of the best summers ever was when Jalin took driver education lessons in Southfield. He stayed with us for several weeks. He got to spend time with his granddad and me. We visited different restaurants. We had the best time taking him to Miller's Bar in Dearborn, Michigan, where you could bring kids for meals before 4:00 p.m. Of course, our grandson called right afterwards and told his parents,"Granddad and Grandma took me to a bar!" They were Seventh-Day Adventists, so they did not eat meat. Eric allowed Jalin to partake of foods that they didn't eat because of their own religious persuasion. We knew that he loved hamburgers, but he didn't eat those at home. He enjoyed one the best burgers in town during that visit. His granddad also introduced him to butter pecan ice cream! Oh my goodness! He loved it! At our house, Blue Bunny Vanilla was the ice cream of choice! We always made sure we kept butter pecan ice cream and rainbow sherbet as well— that was the grandkids' favorite during their visits.

We could not be happier. We had found a way to resolve all of the hurt and pain before the kids got too big and engrossed in their teen activities to enjoy us! It was the best thing ever to have been able to expose our grandchildren to enjoy some of the things we loved so much. I can't imagine having missed all of that just because of bad feelings between Eric and me. It didn't matter anymore that we had not had any honest dialogue. The most important thing was to move forward finally. That was the best decision ever. So many people take their anger to their graves and lose out on so much of the joys of life by holding onto something from the past. It only hurts the person holding on to it. It is never worth clinging to old hurts. Someone has to be the change agent. Someone has to start the dialogue. Seize the day. Tomorrow is not promised.

LESSONS
LEARNED

- Your situation won't change until you decide to make a shift in your thinking.
- There will be no growth if you maintain a victim mentality.
- Focus on what's truly important to you because that will guide you to a positive resolution.

CHAPTER 19

I Thought I Was in My Second Act

"Mom, I often wondered what your life would have been like if you hadn't gotten pregnant, and you were able to fulfill your dream of going to college right after high school," said Eric. Eric knew about the many trials both he and I had gone through during my pregnancy, his birth and the many tests we had to endure. I told him I honestly could not imagine having missed the joy or sorrows of being his mom. His birth and my early challenges shaped us into the strong and able-bodied people we became. It is my pleasure just being a part of the common everyday experiences we share. These precious and sometimes mundane occurrences speak of our healthy relationship. One day out of the blue I got a call from Eric. He got a chance to speak in Bermuda, and he asked if I had my passport. He wanted to take me along because it was a presentation about education and the role parents played in their child's development. After all our hardships, this invite was more precious than gold! That was the first time I saw him do his work. And at some point, I was asked to speak as well! I thought, "Be still my heart. My son is asking me to speak at a forum on parenting! There is a God!" I also had the pleasure of watching him work in Miami at a Nike sponsored event. From there we hopped on another plane to meet the Phoenix Suns. These trips blessed me. I was able to witness first-hand the power that my son's life altering speeches had on his audiences. I became one of his ardent fans as well, and I began to follow his weekly TGIM videos. It's funny, but he became my teacher through the videos. I began to grow spiritually and emotionally. Eric has allowed me to travel to England and Australia to attend the conferences with him and the Squad as well as events across America! I felt like a member of ETA.

As his company grew, I would often get calls from his HR rep who would ask for my advice on business and HR matters. It seemed he often spoke of the business skills I got working in the corporate arena for 30+ years. I was told that Eric told them to reach out to me if they had questions regarding business matters. I was flattered that he would consider me as a resource. One day while my husband and I were on vacation I received a call from Eric's HR manager; she asked if I would be interested in a part-time job at ETA.

Of course I said yes. They offered me a job without Eric knowing about it. When he found out they had hired me, Eric was shocked, but the young lady defended herself by stating that he always asked her to reach out to me for help. The Company needed a part-time worker. Eric stated that he wasn't concerned about my business savvy, but he was a little concerned that my strong personality could be a hindrance as I was manning 2 phone lines. He conceded and said, "Mom, I'm going to give you 90 days to see how you work out."

Every couple of weeks he proclaimed, and I would say, "You know you have to make me a permanent employee after 89 days!"

His response would always be, "I haven't received any complaints, so I'm going to give you a 30 day extension." I told him that he better fire me before my 90 days are up or he will be stuck with me! I had a great career at Ford Motor Company, but working for my son and in the capacity of interacting with his fans and supporters who call seeking advice, gave me a renewed spirit. I was able to work with using my strength in being a listening ear. Being a part of the ETA Squad was my best second act.

Mother to Mother:
Something Ain't Always Better than Nothing
Those storms of defeat—and yes, even heartbreak—can give you the fire you need to push yourself to greatness. I made it off the welfare rolls before Eric was two years old. I managed because I had a purpose and a plan to execute it within a predetermined time frame. I had watched my mother struggle with thirteen kids as a mostly single parent, and she was pregnant with her fourteenth. Her two marriages had failed, and our fathers, for the most part, had dropped off the face of the earth. When I finally gave birth to my own son, I couldn't imagine not having some kind of help from my son's father, so I didn't sever our ties even though I knew our relationship was damaged beyond repair.

Many of us make excuses for ourselves about why we hold on to something we know is toxic. We bend the truth and try to make something redeeming out of something that we know has no redeeming qualities just so we can pretend that we didn't make a mistake in choosing the wrong guy. That way, we can look at ourselves in the mirror and say, " I did not make such a poor character judgment when I chose my boyfriend." Then we won't have to say to ourselves what I didn't want to say to myself, " Everything that I saw in this guy was based on surface."

Because my relationship with Gerald was one dimensional, I could not see the type of person he truly was. My moving too fast with our relationship did not allow me to see his true character. I had fallen for a guy who only saw life as something to be enjoyed for a time. He was a guy who had no true character or redeeming qualities, at least where me and his first born were concerned. As time went on I still had no clue of what I did want, but I knew what I didn't want. I would no longer engage in sex with him, as it would only lead to my falling into a deeper hole. It wasn't in the cards for him and me to go any further; he was not going to be tied down. He wasn't going to stop his wayward ways, and I wasn't going to stay with a man whom I knew wasn't looking for anything with me except sex when it crossed his mind.

One of the hardest things I had to do was finally cut the cord altogether with Gerald and tell him that it was completely over. However, he didn't give up quite so easily. When he finally realized that I was no longer available when he had nothing else to do, he decided to walk away from us both. It clarified everything I had thought about our so-called relationship. It did not matter what I had thought the relationship was. I had thought it was love, but I realized I was looking for love in all the wrong places. What my younger self did not understand was that because my youth was so chaotic, I didn't even know what to look for in a man. I had no real idea of how a real man behaved. All I knew for certain was that I couldn't be with a man who was physically or emotionally abusive. Growing up with my stepfathers, I had seen enough of that. I would not accept that type of disregard. However, at that point, I myself was so emotionally broken that I wouldn't have known a good man if he had fallen into my lap. Although, because I'd seen so many bad men, I was able to recognize Gerald for what he was. Although he might have been a good man for some other woman, our relationship was toxic.

Some time after Gerald left for good, I had the good fortune to meet Jesse. I had grown, and I started to act by principles rather than my feelings with respect to my own self-development and character. I looked at life on a deeper level and not just on the physical level where someone seems attractive because of certain physical attributes. I was able to recognize character. We can't make better choices about the people with whom we choose to interact with until we first self-assess. We must acknowledge and work to eliminate our own flaws, and we must have the desire to be better emotionally.

We attract what we are. Had I not grown emotionally, spiritually, and socially, I would have continued to choose someone with Gerald's character. However, after we broke up, I turned inward and focused on myself and my son. I did not worry about having a man, which was what had almost brought me to my knees. I had no need to repeat that situation. I never focused on marrying because Eric was my number one responsibility. My obligation was to see that he had the best life I could give him. I wanted to do it without all the distractions and drama that can come with being a single mother and having to introduce my son to new men that would be allowed to enter into our lives. I had to be mindful and sure.

You can't enter a new relationship just for yourself. If you haven't learned a valuable lesson with the birth and breakup with your child's father, you are bound to repeat the same mistakes. Without reflecting on how you found yourself in that position, you will attract the same type of character. Your future relationships will bring about the same results if you are not able to identify your weaknesses when attracting another partner. Entering another unstable relationship can potentially create pain for your child, as they can become emotionally connected to that partner. And when the relationship ends, the cycle starts over again.

LESSONS
LEARNED

- Be honest and take responsibility for choosing the person you entered into a relationship with.
- Look inward to understand why you make the choices you make.
- Own up to your part in it.
- Stop the blame game.
- Without your honest assessment, you will continue to attract that same character-type.
- I was attracted to my son's father because of my own brokenness.
- Only when we understand and work on and through our weaknesses, can we attract and be attracted to a person with great character.

"When I stand before God at the end of my life, I would hope I would not have a single bit of talent left and I could say, I used everything you gave me. "
— **Erma Bombeck**

EPILOGUE

The Best is Yet to Come

The best is yet to come!

My Third Act is on the horizon! From where I can sit now this is just the beginning of a totally new journey. God only knows where it will lead me, but I am strapped in and ready!

My son asked me to write this book, and I was so happy that he was behind me sharing my story through my lenses. I wanted people to see my perspective during those years as a young mother. I wanted them to know how I managed to take my messes and create a masterpiece. I was truly blessed when I changed my mindset and finally understood Eric's viewpoint on how everything played out regarding his birth and subsequent adoption. It was as real as my own viewpoint of how I processed it.

My going to college was delayed, and it took me more than 12 years to finish. During those times, I was juggling married life, children, work and setbacks, but I managed to complete my BA in Business Administration just before my youngest daughter Mallori walked the stage for her undergrad college degree. I look for-ward to sharing my journey with you so you can see that the sky's the limit if you just make the decision to put your dreams into play with that first step. If you do that, I promise you will arrive just where you want to be. I double dare you to set your bar high because wherever you want to be, it's possible to get there if you have the faith that you are going to make it! Be determined that no matter how many times you fall you will pick yourself up and get back in that game called life.

ERIC THOMAS AND ASSOCIATES, LLC.

EDUCATION CONSULTING | ATHLETIC DEVELOPMENT | EXECUTIVE COACHING | PROFESSIONAL DEVELOPMENT

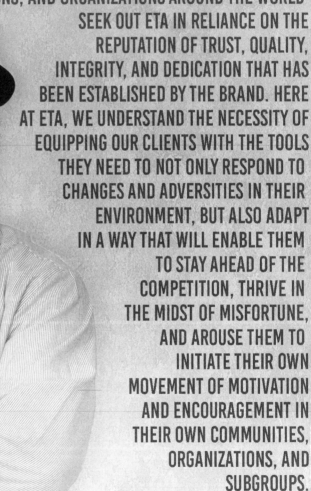

"WHEN YOU WANT TO SUCCEED AS BAD AS YOU WANT TO BREATHE..."
EDUCATORS, CORPORATIONS, AND ORGANIZATIONS AROUND THE WORLD SEEK OUT ETA IN RELIANCE ON THE REPUTATION OF TRUST, QUALITY, INTEGRITY, AND DEDICATION THAT HAS BEEN ESTABLISHED BY THE BRAND. HERE AT ETA, WE UNDERSTAND THE NECESSITY OF EQUIPPING OUR CLIENTS WITH THE TOOLS THEY NEED TO NOT ONLY RESPOND TO CHANGES AND ADVERSITIES IN THEIR ENVIRONMENT, BUT ALSO ADAPT IN A WAY THAT WILL ENABLE THEM TO STAY AHEAD OF THE COMPETITION, THRIVE IN THE MIDST OF MISFORTUNE, AND AROUSE THEM TO INITIATE THEIR OWN MOVEMENT OF MOTIVATION AND ENCOURAGEMENT IN THEIR OWN COMMUNITIES, ORGANIZATIONS, AND SUBGROUPS.

THE ETA METHOD IS COMPRISED OF THREE ESSENTIAL THREADS:

STEP 1 - SEED → STEP 2 - GROW → STEP 3 - INSPIRE

ONE-ON-ONE COACHING WITH ET EMAIL COACHING@ETINSPIRES.COM

WELCOME TO

BREATHE UNIVERSITY™

JOIN ERIC THOMAS INSIDE BREATHE UNIVERSITY TODAY AND DISCOVER THE BATTLE-TESTED AND PROVEN KNOWLEDGE, TOOLS, AND SUPPORT YOU NEED TO ACHIEVE YOUR GREATEST GOALS AND DREAMS STARTING NOW.

A HOLISTIC APPROACH TO SUCCESS, INVOLVING A SERIES OF INTIMATE INSTRUCTIONAL SESSIONS WITH INSPIRATIONAL SPEAKER AND LIFE STRATEGIST, DR. ERIC THOMAS. STUDY ALONG WITH HIM AS HE DELIVERS STRATEGIES ON HOW YOU CAN MOVE FROM WHERE YOU ARE TO WHERE YOU KNOW YOU SHOULD BE THROUGH VIDEOS, MP3S, COMMUNITY DISCUSSION GROUPS, ACCESS TO LIVE Q&A'S FACILITATED BY ERIC, AND OTHER TOOLS AND RESOURCES THAT YOU CAN USE TO HELP TRANSFORM YOUR LIFE IN THE AREAS OF: FINANCE, RELATIONSHIPS, CAREER GOALS MARRIAGE AND MORE...

WHEN YOU WANT TO SUCCEED AS BAD AS YOU WANT TO

BREATHE UNIVERSITY™

DISCOVER YOUR STORY, ENROLL NOW.

ONE-ON-ONE
VIDEO COURSES

FOR MORE INFORMATION OR QUESTIONS ABOUT BREATHE UNIVERSITY™ OR THE COURSE OFFERINGS PLEASE CONTACT INFO@BREATHEUNIVERSITY.COM OR CALL US AT 866-526-3978 EXT.4.

PUBLICATIONS